Unexpected Journey

*From the life as a country black youth,
to the highest army enlisted rank,
to a Senior Pastor.*

Silas Swint

SILAS SWINT

Unexpected Journey

Copyright © 2025 by Silas Swint
All rights reserved.

This is a work of nonfiction. All events and experiences are based on the author's true life and are presented to the best of his memory and interpretation.

First Edition
Published by Book Writing League

For more information, visit:
www.SilasBooks.com

ISBN: 978-1-965408-67-4

Published By
Book Writing League
www.bookwritingleague

Dedication

This book is dedicated to everyone who has ever been told that their dreams were out of reach.

To those who were blamed for the hardships they endured in their youth, and to those who gave up on pursuing their passions because they believed they weren't qualified—May this work serve as a reminder that your worth is not defined by others' expectations, and that it's never too late to rise, to believe, and to move forward with purpose.

Table of Contents

Foreword

The chapters in this book are not intended to follow a strict chronological or sequential order, although some may naturally do so. Instead, they focus on a series of momentous events in my life. Each event may include follow-ups and ongoing developments, reflecting how these experiences evolved over time. This story aims to illustrate how, unknowingly, I was being prepared for the journey that has brought me to where I am today. I hope it offers both an engaging narrative and insight into why this journey has been so unexpected.

Initially, I had planned to connect the story to the namesake of Fort Hood, Texas. However, with the recent renaming of the fort to Fort Cavazos, that connection has shifted in relevance. Although ties to the original namesake, John Bell Hood, still exist, the urgency to pursue that connection has diminished. I apologize for the delay in completing this work—other events and circumstances have taken precedence.

After retiring from active ministry, I anticipated having more downtime. However, that hasn't been the case. Managing household responsibilities and supporting the production of documents for various projects have occupied much of my time. I have also served as the IT support for my wife's Women's Missionary Society ministry, assisting with computer and internet tasks.

Chapter 1
Early Years

I was born in Sandersville, Washington County, Georgia, on October 10, 1947, to Charlotte Burnic Swint and Cosby Thomas. At the time of my birth, my mother lived somewhere along Highway 15, also known as Worthen Highway. When I was two years old, our family moved to a house on Jordan Mill Road, owned by the Wright family. The road was named after the nearby Jordan Mill, which processed raw corn into cornmeal.

At four years old, we relocated to another house about a mile away, owned by the Olin Trussell family. This move marks my earliest long-term memory—I vividly recall walking from the old house to the new one.

The new house was a typical farmhouse for that era, without electricity or running water. There was a dug well beside the front porch for water. Living on land owned by others meant we were sharecroppers—a subject I'll discuss more later. The house had two bedrooms, a kitchen, a storage room, and a small front porch. Since there was no indoor plumbing, we had no toilet or bathroom. For lighting, we used kerosene lamps. A fireplace provided warmth, and we cooked on an iron stove that burned wood.

There were six of us living in the house: three brothers, one sister, my mother, and me. As time went on, one brother got married and moved out. Another sister was born later, and eventually, another brother got married and left as well. Eventually, it was just my mother, two sisters, one brother, and me living in the house. My older sister also married and moved out later.

I began my education at a rural school called **Royal Junior High School**. If I walked to school, it was about half a mile through the woods. Taking the bus, however, meant a two-mile trip. I attended this school until the middle of sixth grade, when it closed, and we were bused four miles into town to attend a newly built, consolidated school. Unlike the rural school, which lacked running water and indoor toilets, the new school had all the modern facilities of the time.

Living in the countryside meant there wasn't much to do for entertainment. We played the usual children's games, such as hide-and-seek and hopscotch, and invented others as well. The boys often went on "discovery trips," wandering down dirt roads and exploring the nearby forests. We climbed trees and found various berries, nuts—especially hickory—and fruits like persimmons along the way.

I grew up in a Christian household, and we attended a Baptist church. The church was about three miles away, and without a car, we had to walk there. Daytime services were manageable, but revival services, which ended after dark, posed a challenge. Sometimes we walked home in the dark; other times, we carried a flashlight. Regardless of the situation, I believe God watched over us—none of us were ever bitten by a snake.

Everyone went into town on Saturdays to buy groceries. The children walked, while my mother paid someone to drive her and bring her back with the groceries. Although groceries could be bought during the week, all stores closed at noon on Wednesdays—though I don't recall why. On Sundays, no stores were open at all. As teenagers, we would stay in town until dark and dance at local short-order eateries, which we called **juke joints.** If we couldn't get a ride, we'd walk the four miles back home in the dark. It might sound crazy, but it was the only time we had for socializing, fun, and enjoyment—and I have to say, I was quite the dancer!

I don't believe I've mentioned this before, but my early life was spent below the poverty line. Sharecropping generally meant living in poverty unless you had another source of income beyond farm work. For a time, my second and third oldest brothers worked in the logging business, locally known as "pulpwood." Their income helped, but when they got married and moved out, we fell deeper below the poverty line.

Without electricity, we relied on kerosene lamps for lighting at night. In winter, we used the fireplace for warmth, which meant going into the woods to gather firewood. Even I had to help chop and haul wood. For cooking, we used a wood-burning stove. If we could afford it, we bought firewood, but when money was tight, we had to search the woods for it. I still remember doing my homework by the light of those kerosene lamps.

Chapter 2
Education

As I mentioned earlier, I began school at Royal Junior High School at the age of five. The school term started in September. Typically, students were required to be six years old to enroll, but since my birthday was in October, I was permitted to start early.

My first-grade teacher was Mrs. Willie Mae Rhodes, who became a pivotal influence in my life. We came from a family with very limited financial means, so money was scarce. We often brought our lunch from home, which usually consisted of peanut butter and saltine cracker sandwiches.

One of the first significant ways Mrs. Rhodes impacted my life happened during lunch one day. A boy in my class didn't have any lunch and wanted mine. When I refused to give it to him, he knocked my food to the ground. Since the ground was dirty and crawling with ants, the food was no longer edible. Mrs. Rhodes witnessed what happened and paddled the boy for his behavior. The next day, his older sister came to the school and attacked Mrs. Rhodes. In self-defense, Mrs. Rhodes bit her. I don't know what became of the sister, but the boy never bothered me again after that incident.

I did very well in elementary school. With few extracurricular activities, I had plenty of time to study. However, my academic success attracted jealousy from other students. My teacher often asked me to explain mathematical fractions on the blackboard, which only worsened my relationship with my peers. The dreaded label of "teacher's pet" was frequently directed at me. And if I made even one mistake, insults would start flying. But I let the comments slide off me because I knew I could still outperform most of them. This wasn't arrogance or being "stuck-up"; it was my way of compensating for the low self-esteem I felt due to living in poverty.

When the new school was ready, Royal Junior High School closed, and I transferred midway through the sixth grade. To my surprise, my homeroom teacher at the new school was none other than Mrs. Willie Mae Rhodes, my first-grade teacher. Since she remembered me, she gave me the responsibility of being the lunch ticket monitor.

As part of my duties, I collected lunch money from students, recorded their names, and went to the office to get the lunch tickets. This task became another pivotal moment in my life. By now, it was clear that my family was poor—or, as some would say, poverty-stricken. I didn't have lunch money, and the cost of lunch was twenty cents. However, for every ten paid lunches, the school provided three free lunch tickets. Mrs. Rhodes knew my situation and entrusted me with deciding who would receive those free tickets. Naturally, I kept one for myself and selected two other students to receive the remaining tickets.

As I mentioned before, Mrs. Rhodes played a key role in my life, and her kindness and trust left a lasting impact on me—not just once, but multiple times.

For my seventh-grade year, I had a new homeroom teacher named Ms. Majors. She didn't know anything about me—my background or my financial situation. I still didn't have money to buy lunch, so I stayed in the homeroom during lunch breaks. That worked for a while.

Ms. Majors sold candy bars, and it didn't take long for her to figure out why I wasn't going to lunch. Occasionally, she would give me a candy bar. That was fine until the other students found out. They didn't take it well. At the time, I was smaller than most kids in my grade, and things quickly escalated. It wasn't just teasing—they were bullying me. Both boys and girls took part. They made up stories about things I supposedly did and used that as an excuse to start fights.

I couldn't beat the boys in fights, but I always fought back. When it came to the girls, it was even worse. If I tried to defend myself, they would scream as if I were attacking them. Despite the odds, I stood my ground. I was never the one to start fights, but when faced with no choice, my fight-

or-flight instinct kicked in. And when I had no room to walk away, that's when the "mouse became a man."

Nothing particularly notable happened after that until high school. Much of my curiosity and thirst for knowledge were driven by experiences during puberty and adolescence, which I'll discuss in a later chapter.

In high school, I heard plenty of warnings about a strict teacher named Ms. Pearson. Everyone said, "When you get to high school, make sure you don't get Ms. Pearson." Well, guess what—I got Ms. Pearson. That was my fate. She was a tough, no-nonsense teacher, and we were terrified of her. One day in class, a girl flirted with me, and I flirted back. Ms. Pearson caught us, and she lost it. She shouted, "Vulgar behavior!" I thought I was done for. She stood up as if she was going to take serious action, but then she sat back down. I think my A-average in her class may have influenced her decision to let it slide. Either way, I was relieved when that term ended.

Then came a day I'll never forget—November 22, 1963. Several teachers were crying, and at first, I had no idea why. Later, I learned that President John F. Kennedy had been assassinated. I couldn't fully process the gravity of it at the time. However, looking back, I believe that this event sparked my interest in political science. It affected me deeply, especially because one of the teachers who was crying was Mrs. Scott, my former French teacher, with whom I had a personal connection.

As an introvert, I didn't have many friends. In fact, two people I thought were my friends turned out to be anything but. They were what I now recognize as "frenemies." Throughout school, I focused on doing the best I could. While my family's socio-economic situation wasn't ideal, I took great pride in my academic abilities. I never bragged about it; I just kept working hard.

Toward the end of the school year, I discovered that two of these so-called friends were jealous of my academic performance. They conspired to steal one of my books and hide it. At the time, shorthand was still a subject taught in high school, along with typing, and I was excelling in both. I had the highest grade in the class, but after my book disappeared, my grades suffered. They were delighted to see my average drop.

Then, just before the end of the semester, the missing book mysteriously reappeared on my desk. This happened near the end of our senior year, so fortunately, I didn't have to deal with them anymore. Despite their efforts, I still graduated with honors.

The two conspirators weren't even from my hometown—they came from a neighboring town, as the high school served the entire county. I won't dignify them by mentioning their names. It's astonishing what some people will do to try to block your destiny. What they didn't realize is that while they may have caused delays, they could not change what God had ordained. It is during such trials that you learn who your true friends are—and who your "frenemies" are.

After graduating from high school, I enrolled at Fort Valley State University. Unfortunately, things didn't go as planned. My student loan request was denied, and after the first quarter, I had no choice but to return home. Not long after, I received a notice informing me that the denial had been a mistake and that I could return to school. I did—but the administration made another error, and I once again found myself without the financial support I needed to continue. I stayed through Christmas break, but by January, I was fed up with the back-and-forth. I decided not to return for the second semester and chose to change my career path.

In April 1966, I began my service in the United States Army. I'll talk about my army career in another section, but for now, I'll continue with the story of my education.

While stationed at Fort McClellan, Alabama (now known by a different name), I resumed my studies at Gadsden State University. Later, when I was assigned to Fort Hood, Texas (now Fort Cavazos), I continued my education at Central Texas College, where I earned an Associate Degree in General Studies. I chose this degree because it allowed me to transfer my previous credits.

After completing my military career, I decided to become a full-time student at the University of Mary Hardin-Baylor in Belton, Texas. Several factors motivated me to go back to school and earn my bachelor's degree. After retiring from the military, I took a few months off—from August to November—before I began looking for a job. Someone suggested I check with the local Independent School District for a position as an aide, and I did just that. I was hired as a Level II Aide in Special Education, and before long, I was promoted to Level III Aide.

While working as a Level III Aide, I witnessed something that deeply disturbed me. Some teachers intentionally provoked students into acting out so they could have them removed from their classrooms. This behavior troubled me greatly.

During my next evaluation meeting with the school district, I was asked if I had anything to share in confidence. I told them what I had observed. The evaluator then told me that one way I could make a real difference was to go back to school, earn my teaching degree, and return as a certified teacher. That idea resonated with me, and I decided to pursue it.

I applied to the University of Mary Hardin-Baylor and was accepted. Initially, I intended to study mathematics, but I quickly encountered a challenge. In high school, I had been discouraged from taking trigonometry, which left a gap in my math knowledge. That gap made it difficult for me to transition into higher-level college math. Linear Algebra, in particular, proved to be my breaking point. I realized that I needed to change my academic focus if I wanted to move forward without starting over completely.

Since I wanted to build on my existing credits, I switched to a Bachelor of General Studies. My two main fields of study became Business Administration and Computer Information Systems. The latter was heavily focused on computer science and programming. I completed the entire programming curriculum required for a degree in computer science, though the structure of my program didn't allow me to earn that degree specifically.

I graduated with a bachelor's degree in General Studies, along with certifications to teach Business Administration and Computer Information Systems. Structuring the degree this way allowed me to transfer credits from both military coursework and previous academic institutions. I made the Dean's List for two semesters, with my studies primarily focused on computer science and programming.

Several of my programming professors tried to recruit me to work for McClain Enterprises as a software developer. However, I turned down the opportunity without hesitation. After spending a career in the military, I had no desire to enter the cutthroat corporate world of "dog-eat-dog" competition. My heart was set on teaching high school students, and I stayed true to that goal.

To earn full certification as a teacher, I had to complete both student teaching and an additional education course after graduation. When it came time to take my graduation photos, there was a bit of confusion about my status. I later discovered that the photographer mistakenly dressed me in a master's degree gown. I wasn't aware of it at the time, but it certainly made for an amusing memory.

I did my student teaching at Killeen High School in Killeen, Texas. One challenge I quickly noticed was the disconnect between what I had learned in college and what was being taught in high schools. For instance, I learned the C programming language in college, but high schools had already moved on to C++. Even though I was certified to teach, I realized I had to learn C++ on my own to keep up. So, I bought *C++ For Dummies*. Despite the title, the book was surprisingly effective, and since C++ builds on C, it wasn't too difficult for me to grasp.

There's an important detail I need to include here. To become certified in Texas, I had to pass state exams in both of my major fields of study. The Business Administration test was straightforward, and I passed it without issue. However, the computer science exam presented a unique challenge. The programming language covered in the test was no longer taught in college—a frustrating gap between the curriculum, state certification, and the school system's needs.

Once again, *C++ For Dummies* became my go-to study guide, but this time it only helped to a certain extent. I took the computer science exam three times, missing the passing score by just two or three points each time. I began to feel discouraged, thinking that perhaps teaching computer science wasn't meant to be. I had temporarily forgotten that I wasn't in this alone.

So, I turned to prayer. I said, "Lord, if it is Your will for me to teach computer programming, help me to pass this test." I let it go and put it in God's hands. I stopped studying and preparing altogether. And then, just like that, I passed the exam and became certified to teach Computer Science.

For the next nine years, I taught Computer Science, Digital Graphics, and Video Technology at C.E. Ellison High School in Killeen, Texas. It's funny—growing up, I never imagined myself becoming a teacher or having a military career. Life had other plans for me. This was all part of what I now call my *Unexpected Journey*.

Before moving on, I need to share a situation where an attempt was made to interfere with this path. Two teachers tried to manipulate my position by asking if I preferred to teach regular Computer Programming or AP (Advanced Placement) Computer Programming. I responded that I'd prefer teaching regular programming. However, they twisted my words and told the principal that I refused to teach AP classes.

The principal called me into his office and told me that if I didn't want to teach AP Programming, I couldn't remain at the school. I clarified what had really happened and asked him who had reported this misinformation. After he told me, I explained the full conversation and assured him that I was willing to fulfill whatever my contract required.

After leaving the principal's office, I prayed again. I told God, "If I need to confront this person, let them be in their office when I get there. If they aren't there, I'll take it as a sign that You've already handled it." When

I arrived at their office, they weren't there. I knew then that God had answered my prayer.

In the end, the other computer teacher, who had wanted my position, was transferred to a different high school.

Teaching AP Computer Science required continuous professional development. To stay updated with programming advancements, AP teachers were expected to attend a two-week seminar hosted by Carnegie Mellon University. These sessions were held on the campus of the University of North Texas in Dallas, Texas. The seminar provided invaluable reference materials and new ideas to incorporate into the curriculum, ensuring that we kept our courses relevant and up to date.

The seminar was conducted entirely by the Carnegie Mellon Institute, whose instructors seemed more interested in playing volleyball in the 100-degree Texas heat than teaching. I suppose, coming from the cooler northern part of the country, they enjoyed the heat. I, however, declined to participate.

During the seminar, we were introduced to the next major programming language—Java. While JavaScript had already been in use, Java was new to us. It shared similarities with C++ in its use of functions but added conversational elements, making it more versatile and powerful. We spent a significant amount of time learning Java, and we were even offered the opportunity to purchase additional lessons on a CD.

I returned home eager to dive into this newly adopted programming language and apply what I had learned. However, in early August, I received an unexpected call from the principal's office. I was informed that Computer Science had been removed from the curriculum at the direction of the Texas Education Agency (TEA). Instead, I was now required to teach *Technology Applications*, with subjects that included **Digital Graphics** and **Video Technology**.

This sudden change required a major adjustment, both mentally and academically. To make matters more challenging, there was no pre-existing curriculum for these courses. I had to not only create the curriculum from scratch but also align it with the pre-packaged software that the district had already purchased for these subjects.

The lack of guidance from TEA meant I had to rely heavily on my own research skills. I spent countless hours conducting online research to develop notebooks with suggested guidelines and recommendations for creating effective curricula in Digital Graphics and Video Technology. These materials served as a blueprint for structuring the new courses.

During teacher preparation week, before the students returned, I was called to the Superintendent's Office for a meeting. The Superintendent and Assistant Superintendent wanted to discuss my proposed plans for the new classes. They asked me to bring the notebooks I had assembled. After briefly reviewing my materials, they commended my research efforts.

At this meeting, based on my recommendations and additional input, the district made an important decision: they allocated $150,000 to each high school to equip the new classrooms for Digital Graphics and Video Technology.

In addition to my teaching career, I also pursued theological studies at Fuller Theological Seminary, where I completed 33 units of coursework. This period of theological studies, along with my time at the University of Mary Hardin Baylor and teacher certification, all followed the completion of my military career. I will share more about my military journey in another chapter.

Chapter 3
Interpersonal and
Environmental Impact.

This section is difficult to discuss. It may be challenging for some to read, but it's also cathartic to share. There was a time when I couldn't talk about this part of my life. These experiences profoundly shaped who I became. Of course, it was a process of overcoming what happened to me. If you choose to read this section, you'll understand.

Many people have encountered or read "coming-of-age" stories, which often involve sexual awakening. Now that you know the topic, you may decide to skip ahead. However, I want to tell the whole story. It might help others understand what can happen in life and how we can overcome trauma.

I considered never saying anything about this experience. But then I thought, what if someone goes through these things and feels that it's too much to overcome? Someone who finds themselves broken because of what has happened to them, which they didn't cause, or perhaps they think it might be their fault. So let me be blunt: nothing that an adult or older person has done to you sexually when you were a child or adolescent is your fault. Period. End of story.

I'm a prolific reader, and I've seen how this kind of traumatic experience can affect different people. But getting back to my story, yes, I was sexually touched by two different adult males as a pubescent and adolescent. There was no physical harm to my body. However, there was harm done to my mind, my psyche, and my self-esteem. At that time, the offenses were called sexual abuse and carnal knowledge.

The sexual abuse part was damaging because I had to deal with it alone. I was too young to know what to do with the information. So, yes, the burden was to keep it to myself. Really, I just thought it was something that happened in life.

18

As for the carnal knowledge part, that's what affected me the most. Before this began to happen to me, all I was interested in learning about were the things taught in school and the books we were assigned. But after this new experience, I wanted to know all about sexual things. I would study the dictionary. I would read anything that contained anything that referenced things of a sexual nature. I had a hunger for sexual knowledge. I didn't wish to do these things, but I wanted to know about them and why people did them. I even heard about some other teenagers in our community who said they knew about people who did sexual things with animals. I didn't believe that those things happened. Then I learned about bestiality. I subsequently found out that it's also mentioned in scripture.

Even though I appeared the same physically, the unseen parts of me were broken. I didn't realize I was broken until I discovered I had trouble having normal relationships with males, especially men. I remember being an extrovert earlier in life. But after the molestation, I became a loner, an introvert. I couldn't be around males because I was afraid of having a sexual reaction.

Now, I can give hugs to both males and females. During my puberty, adolescence, and teenage years, I couldn't touch a male without becoming sexually aroused. I presume it was because my mind had somehow connected all males with the physical reactions during the times of abuse and molestation. I was broken. My mental self, spiritual self, and self-esteem were all broken. I became fearful of being around males because of the possibility of an embarrassing situation. So, unless I had to be around people, I spent a lot of time alone.

In my late teens, I even considered suicide. At that time, I only knew of painful methods. Ironically, I was afraid of pain! I remember when the clinic staff came to school to give immunizations. I resisted so much that a heavy woman had to step on my feet to keep me still while administering the shot.

Because I wasn't aware of any other way to end my life, I didn't follow through with the idea. I didn't know about, nor did I have access to, medications that could have ended my life. I've come to understand that it wasn't my decision to not carry this out. There was divine intervention to prevent me from doing it. And because I went through this, I received the gift and ability to help others who have had similar experiences.

There may be something to the adage, "What doesn't kill you makes you stronger." This helped me become who I am and gave me the strength to stand in the gap for others. I've been able to share what I've been through, and yet people see the grace of God in me. I won't reveal the names of the perpetrators. Since they were adults when I was a child, they're likely deceased now.

So, how did I become whole again? It took time. My high school teachers played an important role. They challenged me in a way that pushed me to be "out front," so to speak. I asked questions to show my knowledge and intelligence, which gave me the opportunity to show my value to others. This helped me rebuild my self-esteem and self-worth. It helped me see that although I had to do things against my will, I was still the same person I was before. It helped me know that even though things happened to me, those things didn't define me. I was who I was, but I had to compartmentalize those experiences to avoid being mentally and spiritually bound.

There was a wife and mother in our community whom I truly admired. I admired her because she was always in control of her emotions. I watched how she dealt with different emotions and thought, "Wow, I want to be able to do that." So, I practiced. It helped me to put things in perspective, to not be overly concerned by trivial matters, and to move beyond unpleasant experiences. However, the negative effect was that I started to become unemotional. I seldom reacted to any kind of stimuli. I remained this way until I truly accepted God's plan for my life and allowed Him to lead and direct me. It was then that I began to heal. As I learned about His will and His plans for me, I discovered that whatever my shortcomings were, they weren't big enough to interfere with what God wanted to do through me. His grace is sufficient in all things. The strength of God manifested itself in my weakness. A caveat to this is that we don't know when we ourselves will be looked upon as role models and examples to others.

Our economic status was that of sharecroppers. As such, we didn't own anything other than our household belongings. A landowner owned the house and the land. One of my brothers became an overseer. I mentioned that my sister and I had to harvest squash before leaving for school. Being sharecroppers didn't mean we shared in the profits from the sale of the crops. It meant that the landowner planted the crops, and we, who lived on his land, harvested them to prepare them for market. This was a burdensome task. For the squash, we also had to wash and clean them. In earlier years, when most of my family was still at home, we also harvested cotton. Despite the demanding work, we acquired a strong work ethic. This proved to be a valuable asset later in our professional lives. Once ingrained, this characteristic can be applied to any situation.

After finishing our assigned harvesting tasks, we could hire ourselves out to do other farm work. During summer break, my older sister and I hired ourselves out to chop cotton, pick peas, and pick cotton. Chopping cotton had to be done twice: first to thin out the plants and second to clear away weeds and grass. The workday was from 8:00 AM to 6:00 PM, with an hour lunch break. But we were picked up from our house around 7:00 AM. Of course, we had to bring our own lunches. For a day's work, we received a meager $3.00 if we worked for the landowner. Some others paid only $2.00 per day. Yes, I know. But what choice did we have? It was either that or nothing!

The payment for picking peas and cotton was measured by the hundred pounds. For peas, it was $1.00 per hundred pounds harvested. For cotton, it was $1.25 per hundred pound harvested. Peas are much heavier than cotton, which is why the pay ratio was lower for peas. Since the only other household income was a $15.00 stipend every two weeks, my sister and I used our earnings to buy school clothes, hoping for at least three outfits.

I also experienced bailing hay, shucking corn, and plowing the land with a mule. For those unfamiliar, there's a thing called "mule talk." If you used certain words, the mule would understand and respond accordingly. There was a word to tell it to go left, another to tell it to go right, one to tell it to go, and another to tell it to stop. If you didn't know these words, you were in trouble. The pay for plowing with a mule was a whopping $2.00 per day. The man I worked for was also our school bus driver. His wife made breakfast for us. The water came from a dug well that contained mosquito larvae, which we called "wiggle-tails." We had a similar well at our house, right next to the porch. When the spring that fed the well dried up during the dry season, my mother would throw salt into it. I didn't understand why at the time. Later, in school, I learned that salt's chemical property is sodium chloride, and chloride, derived from chlorine, is a purifying agent. I discovered a biblical reference to using salt to purify water.

Most of the peas we picked were purple hull peas. But there was one type called "ladyfingers," or, I think, "cream peas." In my opinion, they were the best-tasting peas. The most traumatic experience of my farm work was picking cotton. I had a fear of worms, and I don't know why. Perhaps it was because we had three types of pecan trees in our yard. Gypsy moths would lay their eggs on the branches, covering them in a web-like substance. After a few weeks, the larvae would hatch and grow. When they matured into worms, they would all fall to the ground at once, crawling everywhere, even into the house and the well. I don't remember if they stung, but I was afraid of them. This is called scoleciphobia.

So, back to the *"cotton-picking trauma."* It could refer to the physical act of picking cotton or the unpleasant experience itself. Insects that attack cotton plants include the boll weevil and the bollworm. The boll weevil didn't bother me, but the bollworm was another story. I didn't like picking cotton when the leaves were still green, but I had no choice. There's an old saying, "grin and bear it," but I certainly didn't grin. I just had to endure it. And if a worm got on my clothes, I'd have to take them off to get rid of it.

Chapter 4
Family Life

I begin this section by sharing my understanding of family and ancestry. We do not choose the family we are born into, nor can we change who our family and ancestors are. We can deny it all we want, but that does not alter the truth. Sometimes, when we discover certain details about our family tree, we may prefer to keep them hidden. However, I believe it is what it is. I had no control over it; it is simply a part of my history. If others have issues accepting me because of it, that is their problem, not mine. I am neither proud nor ashamed of it—it is just a collection of proven and verified facts.

There was a time when slavery existed, lasting for 246 years. It is also a fact that some slave owners and their children fathered children with enslaved women.

With that context, I will now share part of my family history as I know it, based on research confirmed by Ancestry.com.

My mother, Charlotte Burnic Hood, was born to James Hood and Emma Poole Hood. Her siblings were Dora Hood, Rosa Hood, Eula Hood, Mamie Hood, Julian Hood, James Hood Jr., Effie Donnie Hood, Nolan Hood, and twins Jimmie and Zimmie Hood.

Now, here is where things may be considered controversial. As I mentioned earlier, the information I'm sharing comes from family oral history passed down through my mother, grandfather, and other relatives, as well as verification through Ancestry.com.

James Hood Sr., my grandfather, was the son of Dred Hood and Lizzie Hood. Dred Hood's parents were John 2 Hood and Aliza Poole Scott. John 2 Hood has been identified and confirmed as the same person as John Bell Hood. His parents were Sherrod Hood and Nancy Renfro Hood.

Emma Poole Hood, my grandmother, was the daughter of Eddie Allen Poole and Augusta Ann Jordan Poole. Eddie Allen Poole, my great-grandfather, was the son of Robert Poole and Millie R.P. Jones Poole.

It was this same John Bell Hood who first served as an officer in the Union Army but later became a Confederate general. Yes, it was this same John Bell Hood for whom the U.S. Army installation, Fort Hood, Texas, was originally named. However, the installation has since been renamed Fort Cavazos, Texas, as part of an effort to rename all military installations previously named in honor of Confederate generals.

Aliza Poole Scott was a 15-year-old enslaved girl on the Scott Plantation when John 2 Hood, then 21, became involved with her. This union resulted in two sons. While the written history of John Bell Hood mentions two wives and their families, there is little information, apart from census and birth records, about the family he had with Aliza Poole Scott.

My mother, Charlotte Burnic Hood, was married to Harvey Swint. The children from their marriage were Jimmie Dred Swint, Willie Fred Swint, Charlie Swint, and J.B. Swint. My mother also had three other children: Mary Alice Swint Foster, myself, and Ellen Inez Burke. As of this writing, all of my siblings are deceased except Mary and me.

As for my family, I married Mildred Louise (Kinder) Swint at Fort Lee/Petersburg, Virginia, on June 21, 1969. Together, we have three children: Andrette LeVine Swint, Patrick Dion Swint, and Alva Alicia Swint. From them, we have eight grandchildren: Patrick Cordell Swint, Silas Christopher Swint and Marcus Elijah Swint (twins), Antonio Demarcus Swint, Chelsea Gabrielle Swint, Kiera Silese Swint, Keshaun Doe, and Stella Marie Swint. We also have one great-grandchild, Kataleya Silese Doe.

I was present for the births of only two of my children. I flew back from Korea for the birth of our son Patrick, who was born in Anniston, Alabama. Our oldest, Andrette, was born while I was serving in Vietnam. Our youngest, Alva Alicia, was born at Fort Hood, Texas (now Fort

Cavazos, Texas). As fate would have it, Alva Alicia's first child, Kiera, was also born at the same hospital, Darnell Army Hospital, at Fort Hood.

All three of our children graduated from C.E. Ellison High School in Killeen, Texas. We were fortunate to attend all of their high school graduations. Most of our grandchildren who reached high school graduation age have graduated, with one exception. I believe this was due to a failure to properly recognize and address his autistic needs. We attended all of the grandchildren's graduations except for one, who graduated during the abbreviated COVID-19 year.

I was also privileged to attend the college or university graduations of two of my grandchildren. Now, our family is spread across the country, with members living in Texas, Colorado, Florida, and Alabama, as well as Germany.

Chapter 5
Military Life

As I mentioned earlier in this book, I had to leave college due to my financial situation. I did not receive any student loans, nor did I qualify for Work-Study Programs. This failure was partly due to my high school counselors. Yes, they failed me. I did not receive proper advice or guidance about my higher education opportunities. How was I to know about the deadlines and processes for student loan applications and Work-Study Programs? I was quite naïve about what was required before and during registration for higher education.

I had no issue with work. Being accustomed to hard work, I had been working since the age of twelve. My work ethic, responsibility, and accountability were always strong. Hard work was never a problem. We were always taught that anything worth having was worth working for. However, I did not know that my student loan applications had been rejected until Registration Day—imagine that. Home was ninety miles away. After my chaotic first quarter, having been misinformed and misled, I decided this was not my future. On April 19 of the following year, I voluntarily joined the United States Army.

We traveled by bus for 120 miles to Atlanta, Georgia, where the Armed Forces Examination and Entry Station was located. The first thing I noticed was the difference in the taste of the food. Rumors later circulated that this was due to the addition of potassium nitrate (commonly known as saltpeter), which was said to affect the food's flavor. My research shows that potassium nitrate helps build muscle strength and structure. However, the rumor was that it lowered libido. I could not find any verification of this claim; it seemed to be either a conspiracy theory or a joke.

After orientation and indoctrination, I was sent to Fort Benning, Georgia, for Basic Training, which lasted eight weeks. It was challenging for me, particularly in terms of strength and stamina. Sharecropping had not required much strength-building or endurance. I could run fast but not far.

Nevertheless, most of the other recruits were in a similar predicament. I managed to keep up with the others even during double-time, a slow jog for long distances in full combat dress with weapons. Our weapon was the M14A1, which weighed 9.2 pounds unloaded. During double-time, one soldier would pass out and fall almost immediately after we started. He was discharged before completing Basic Training.

One aspect of Basic Training was that we were divided into platoons, each starting with 30 soldiers. Rarely did all 30 remain by the time we graduated. The top ten soldiers received automatic promotion to grade E-2, while the rest of us had to wait a few weeks.

After Basic Training, we were given a two-week break before reporting for Advanced Individual Training (AIT). My AIT was at Fort Eustis, Virginia, which has since been merged with Langley Air Force Base and renamed Joint Base Langley–Eustis. There, I was trained to be a Transportation Movement Control Specialist with a Military Occupation Specialist Code (MOS) of 71N20. This role allowed me to be assigned to any job involving the movement of Army personnel and equipment.

I don't remember whether it was a one-week or two-week break before we had to report for our Permanent Change of Station (PCS). One of the soldiers I attended Basic Training and AIT with invited me to stay overnight at his home so we could fly together to our new assignment. We were both assigned to Japan. He lived in Kennesaw, Georgia, which was closer to Atlanta than my hometown, so I agreed. I remember his stepfather grilling T-bone steaks. They were enormous. It was the first time I had eaten a steak that size, and I couldn't finish it. I wasn't used to eating so much. I was chided for "ruining" a steak, but I responded, "Look at me and my size—you're expecting a miracle here." At the time, I was only 5'8" and weighed 147 pounds.

I believe our flight lasted around 16 hours on Pan American Airlines. We arrived in Tokyo and were then transported by bus to Tachikawa Air Force Base, my new assignment. My soldier friend was later transported to Camp Zama Army Base. My duty was to serve as an Army Air Freight

Coordinator. This role involved ensuring that Army cargo was properly documented and prepared for transport by U.S. Air Force aircraft to its destination. I also had to observe the loading of the cargo onto the airplanes. Tachikawa Air Base couldn't support jet traffic, so the cargo was loaded onto C-124 Globemasters and C-130 Hercules planes using the 463L Pallet System.

Several events stand out from this assignment: experiencing a typhoon, evacuating the barracks due to the discovery of a World War II explosive device, my work situation, and my promotion to Specialist. I'll begin with the typhoon.

For those unfamiliar, a typhoon is a tropical storm in the western Pacific. They are typically larger and stronger than hurricanes due to the vast, warm ocean. This was my first experience with such a storm. Our barracks was well-constructed and soundproof, so I didn't even know a storm had occurred until the next morning. However, some patios and entrance covers had been torn off nearby buildings. Airmen in my barracks mentioned hearing objects being moved around in a room where someone had left a window open. Fortunately, there was no major damage to the base.

The incident with the World War II explosive was a unique experience. We had to evacuate the barracks because of the proximity of the discovered explosive. Later that evening, as it neared time for work, we assumed the emergency had been resolved since we hadn't received any updates. How wrong we were!

When some of us went to change into our uniforms for work, we were apprehended by the Military Police and taken to the station. We were held there for a couple of hours and then released with an admonishment for endangering ourselves. In military terms, it could be described as "a royal chewing out."

We were assigned to work in shifts at the Army ATCO Freight Office. I was not on shift at the time. However, the soldier who was on duty was supposedly swamped with work. I was unaware of this until I came to work on Monday morning and was strongly chastised for not coming in to help.

As a young soldier, this situation was unfamiliar to me. I knew that whenever I was at work, I performed my duties in a professional manner. No fault could be found in my work ethic, so I felt I was being unfairly blamed for something beyond my control. I was emotionally overwhelmed. And yes, since I didn't understand why I was being reprimanded, it brought me to tears.

When I started crying, the person chastising me began to panic, trying to get me to stop before the Officer in Charge entered the office. That reaction told me he knew he was in the wrong. Thankfully, the incident didn't happen again.

Now, about the promotion to Specialist. The promotion to Private First Class was more or less automatic, with no limit on the number of soldiers who could be promoted. However, the promotion to Specialist was different—there was only one slot available, and two of us were eligible. The promotion went to the other soldier, J. Cleveland.

Cleveland and I had gone through Basic Training and AIT together. I was black, and he was white. At the time, I had been taking Correspondence Courses from Fort Eustis related to our MOS, even on topics that extended beyond our specific duties. I credit a Non-Commissioned Officer (NCO), S. Pennington, for encouraging me in this. He was also black and gave me invaluable advice on preparing for a career in the Army.

Pennington understood the reality of the time—that we often had to over-perform to be considered equally for promotion. By successfully completing these courses, I qualified for Proficiency Pay. Despite my efforts and qualifications, I didn't receive the promotion.

When Cleveland was promoted, we congratulated and celebrated with him. However, during the celebration, Cleveland approached me in tears. He apologized, saying he was deeply sorry because he knew I was more qualified for the promotion than he was.

I accepted his apology and assured him it wasn't his fault—he had no control over the decision. I also told him I was confident that when the next promotion slot became available, it would go to me, as I would be the only remaining candidate.

Cleveland continued to express that it wasn't right and that if he could, he would have given me the promotion. Unfortunately, the promotion authority was not stationed with us; they were located more than thirty miles away at Camp Zama.

I was assigned to the Army Air Freight Office at Tachikawa Air Base for two years, and it was one of the most enjoyable assignments of my military career. I was single and a young newbie—eighteen when I arrived and twenty when I left. There were many firsts during this time.

It was the first time I ever drank alcohol and, unsurprisingly, the first time I got intoxicated. We were introduced to a Japanese wine called Akadama, which came with a humorous saying: drinking it would make you "act like a damn fool." That saying wasn't far from the truth! You've probably heard the saying that alcohol brings out your true feelings and personality—witnessed firsthand. If you're harboring secrets, be cautious about who you drink with; getting intoxicated can lead to embarrassing moments or even serious trouble.

While stationed there, I had the chance to visit Tokyo and explore the Ginza, often called one of the greatest shopping and party districts in the world. I also visited various shrines and temples and even got to observe Japanese snow monkeys in their natural habitat. Watching their community relationships was fascinating.

My most memorable trip was to Mount Fuji, or Fujiyama, Japan's most famous mountain. It's a semi-extinct stratovolcano visible from Tachikawa, Tokyo, and much of central Japan. I even climbed part of it, though I had to stop when the air became too thin to continue.

At the office, I served as the courier. My duties included traveling to places like our headquarters at Camp Zama and the Yokohama Naval Base to retrieve documentation. Another first for me was riding a bicycle. Since I needed to ride to the Air Base Message Center to collect documents, some of which were classified, I was issued my own bicycle and courier bag. Riding a bicycle was a new experience for me, and riding on icy streets was an even greater challenge—one I could have done without!

As you saw with the promotion situation earlier, racism at the time was both covert and overt. The overt racism was evident in the local community. Like many military installations, Tachikawa had bars outside the gates, but there was a clear divide. The "Black Gate," or East Gate, was where black soldiers were expected to go, while the "White Gate," or Main Gate, was for white soldiers.

One day, Cleveland invited me to go to a bar with him. When we arrived, one of the bar ladies asked me why I didn't go out the East Gate—a subtle but unmistakable way of saying black men weren't welcome there. I didn't leave, though. Cleveland and I left together at the same time.

During my time there, I also became friends with an Air Force airman from Macon, Georgia. Interestingly, he had a New York accent, which made me think he must have moved to Georgia later in life. After returning to the States, I tried to find him but had no luck.

The next promotion to Specialist Five happened while I was still in Japan, and it came as a complete surprise. I was told to report to the Commander's Office, where all the soldiers from our office were gathered. Everyone was called to attention as the promotion orders were read. Of course, I couldn't stop smiling—it was a proud and unforgettable moment.

My next change of station orders were to Fort Lee, Virginia, which has since been renamed Fort Gregg-Adams in honor of two African American officers: Lt. General Arthur Gregg and Lt. Col. Charity Adams. This assignment was a bit unusual. Although there were Staff Sergeants and Sergeants First Class in the unit, I was converted from Specialist Five to Sergeant and made Platoon Sergeant. Yes, it felt strange. Apparently, they

31

weren't well-versed in Drill and Ceremony. I asked myself how this could happen, but there was no answer.

During my time at Fort Lee, my wife and I were married in one of the chapels. Her uncle and his family drove down from New York, arriving just as the wedding ceremony was ending. It was a wonderful surprise, and we were so happy to see them. At the time of this writing, only one member of that family, one of the daughters, is still alive.

Three other soldiers and I received orders to report to the NCO Academy at Fort Knox, Kentucky. All three of them were Staff Sergeants. I drove to Fort Knox, but the journey was a traumatic experience for me, navigating around and through the mountains of West Virginia. It wasn't enjoyable at all. Thankfully, on the way back, another soldier, more experienced with mountain driving, took the wheel.

While at the academy, I made a significant sacrifice that cost me the honor of being the Top Graduate. I had the highest grade average of all the soldiers attending the academy, but some of the other soldiers from Fort Lee weren't performing well. They appealed to my sense of loyalty and camaraderie, attempting to shame me by saying it would look bad if I excelled while others from Fort Lee failed. They argued that it was important for all of us to graduate together.

I agreed to tutor them, which cut into my own study time and caused my grades to suffer. In the end, we all graduated, which was a good outcome, though I occasionally wondered what might have been if I'd focused solely on my own performance. However, something else positive came out of the experience. While at the academy, I was promoted to Staff Sergeant. Looking back, I believe my willingness to help others was rewarded in the end. Perhaps divine intervention was at play, though I didn't recognize it at the time.

Upon returning to Fort Lee, I was selected to be part of the Color Guard. Our uniform included white helmet liners, white pistol belts, white bootlaces, and Class A uniforms. We performed many Honor Guard details for funerals, as this was during the Vietnam War.

One assignment took me back to West Virginia for a funeral, which was a surprise. I didn't know what to expect of the soldier's family, but I was struck by how much they resembled mine, representing a variety of skin tones and complexions. As the leader of the detail, I wasn't a pallbearer. Instead, I conducted the rifle team, while the Casualty Assistance Officer led the pallbearers.

During the Vietnam War, there were widespread protests, and one tragic incident at a university in Ohio resulted in students being killed. Following that, "Riot Control" forces were no longer issued live ammunition. At Fort Lee, our unit was assigned Riot Control duties. We practiced extensively, armed with bayonets but no live rounds.

Although we were prepared to deploy if needed, we were never called upon, which I greatly appreciated. Despite all our training, there was no way to predict how such a deployment might unfold, and I was relieved that we didn't have to find out.

Following my assignment at Fort Lee, I received orders to deploy to Vietnam. While it wasn't as chaotic as the late 1960s, it was still a dangerous war zone. Our flight lasted seventeen hours, with a refueling stop in the Philippines. We weren't allowed to disembark, so after refueling, we continued to Vietnam, landing at Cam Ranh Bay.

The moment we stepped off the plane, the humidity hit us like a wall. It was so thick it felt as though you could cut it with a knife, combined with an oppressive tropical heat that didn't ease up even after sunset. Even walking to the showers in just underwear felt like being fully dressed. I had never experienced such a climate before.

At Cam Ranh Bay, we waited until we received our in-country assignments. I was flown to Saigon, arriving at Tan Son Nhut Air Base, and from there, I was transported to my final destination: Long Binh Post, the largest Army post in Vietnam. My unit, the 502nd Transportation Detachment, was tasked with assisting in the documentation of equipment being shipped back to the United States.

Our assignments weren't static, so I travelled to various locations across Vietnam, including Cu Chi, Tay Ninh, An Khe, and Ben Thuy. It was at Ben Thuy that I encountered my first deceased soldier. He hadn't been killed in combat but had drowned after falling off a boat during the night. Searching the river in the dark proved fruitless, and it wasn't until three days later that his body surfaced. Seeing how his body had swollen in the water was a harrowing experience that stayed with me.

After some time in the country, the Port of Saigon requested a representative from our unit to help document equipment ready for transport. To my good fortune, I was chosen. However, the only vehicle available for me to drive was a two-and-a-half-ton truck—something I had never driven before. Nevertheless, I was technically licensed to drive it.

You might wonder how that was possible. Well, back then, soldiers were trained on smaller vehicles but often licensed to drive up to five-ton trucks. It's no surprise that accidents were common! Still, I had no choice. Ordered to go alone, I loaded my M16 rifle, summoned my determination, and set off for Saigon (now Ho Chi Minh City), 17 miles away. I kept my horn blaring the entire way to alert the Vietnamese in their three-wheeled vehicles, ensuring they moved out of the path of the "crazy GI." Thankfully, it worked, and I made it safely to my destination.

While stationed at Long Binh Post, I had to serve as Sergeant of the Guard. This role required overcoming my fear of heights, as part of my duties involved climbing a 70-foot guard tower to check on the sentries. Although I had no desire to do it, I had no choice, especially since I had to accompany the Duty Officer.

Vietnam was full of firsts for me, including my first time eating Chinese food. It was delicious, far superior to the fast-food versions we're used to in the States.

When it was time for me to leave Vietnam after completing my tour of duty, I flew out of Bien Hoa Air Base. For safety reasons, we couldn't wear uniforms when arriving back in the United States, as returning service members were often met with hostility. Our flight landed in Spokane,

Washington, where we found ourselves stranded for several hours. Eventually, a plane arrived to take us to Minneapolis-St. Paul, where the airline arranged for us to stay overnight at a hotel near the Mississippi River. I remember waking the next morning to a fresh layer of snow before continuing our journey.

Following Vietnam, my next assignment was to Fort McClellan, Alabama, where I served as a Household Goods Inspector. Our area of responsibility spanned central Alabama, from the Georgia border to the Mississippi border. My duties included inspecting moving companies' packing and shipping practices, documenting and reporting damages to household goods, and processing claims. Each inspector was assigned a pickup truck and a fuel credit card, which allowed us to travel extensively. My work took me to places like Birmingham, Tuscaloosa, Athens, Cullman, Gadsden, Sylacauga, Talladega, Homewood, Jacksonville, and Bessemer. Of course, Anniston and Oxford, near Fort McClellan, were part of my regular territory. Fort McClellan has since been closed.

Next, I was assigned to Camp Casey, South Korea, located in the northern part of the country. Winters there were brutally cold, and the living conditions were less than ideal. For the first six months, I lived in a Quonset hut heated by a five-gallon diesel fuel can at night. Unfortunately, the fuel didn't last until morning, but the cold made it too challenging to refill the heater, so we simply added extra blankets and wore long johns to bed.

Physical training in South Korea was another unique experience. We jogged on ice-covered streets while wearing full combat uniforms. Unsurprisingly, some soldiers slipped and fell, though thankfully, no one sustained serious injuries.

Before receiving orders for South Korea, my specialty underwent a major realignment. I was reclassified into Data Processing and assigned to a newly created unit: the Standard Installation Personnel System (SIDPERS) Interface Branch. This unit was designed to automate personnel reporting systems and assist company commanders with strength reporting and accountability.

As part of this assignment, I was sent on temporary duty to Hawaii to help create a data system for the 2nd Infantry Division. Using punch cards, we built a skeletal database, gradually adding real data to complete individual files for each soldier. This system allowed for both standard and specialized data reporting. It took us three weeks to finish the database.

During this time, my wife and oldest daughter traveled to Hawaii to join me, even though she was pregnant with our son. After completing the database, I returned to South Korea. Later in my assignment, I made another trip to Hawaii with the Officer in Charge to receive additional training in data reporting methods.

This assignment was my introduction to data processing, which would eventually lead to my work in computer programming and the creation of systems to enhance record-keeping and access to current information. Our unit adopted a dragon emblem—a playful nod to the phrase "draggin' them out of the past." Today, it would likely be considered an emoji!

Leaving Korea in 1975, I arrived at my first stateside assignment at Fort Hood, Texas, now renamed Fort Cavazos. Drawing on my experience from building the SIDPERS Interface Branch (SIB), I was assigned to the 2nd Armored Division, 502nd Adjutant General Company, specifically to the SIB. My prior involvement in automating strength accountability and personnel data allowed me to hit the ground running. Initially assigned as a Senior Data Analyst, I was soon promoted to Chief Data Analyst following the retirement of my predecessor. My promotion to Sergeant First Class followed shortly after, as I was already on the promotion list.

At the time, the 2nd Armored Division ranked near the bottom for timely reporting of personnel data. Improving these metrics became my primary task. However, this was complicated by a lack of knowledge and training among unit clerks. To address this, we scheduled battalion-level training sessions to raise awareness of the reporting process. It was crucial that we had the support of the Commanding General and the III Corps

Commander. I worked closely with the III Corps Data Chief to simplify unit-level reporting.

The results were dramatic. We rose from last place to first in on-time reporting, earning recognition throughout the division and from the Department of the Army. Initially, the Division Chief of Staff was concerned that my coordination efforts might undermine the Division Commander's authority. However, my superiors defended my approach, and the success of the program silenced any doubts. The final response from leadership was simply, "Wow."

After six years at Fort Hood, I received orders in 1981 for a new assignment in Germany with concurrent travel for my family. My wife and I traveled with our three children, including our youngest, who was only three months old. According to the rules, one of us had to hold her for the entire flight. Concurrent travel for a Permanent Change of Station (PCS) is supposed to ensure permanent housing within 90 days of arrival, but this was not our experience.

We stayed in two different hotels before housing became available. The first hotel was a particular challenge. The bathroom was located down the hall rather than in our room—a significant inconvenience with a newborn and two young children under the age of ten. We also had to rely on others for transportation to and from the installation, including my daily commute to work. The second hotel was an improvement and closer to the base. Overall, we spent more than a month in temporary accommodations before moving into permanent housing.

This assignment was unique because we were stationed in North Rhine-Westphalia, Germany, an area under the command of the Belgian Army. Our base, Stockerbusch Kaserne, relied on the Belgians for transportation, logistics, and medical support. This introduced a new set of challenges, including the need to learn German for everyday communication and to interact effectively with the Belgian Army.

The Belgian hospital was located in Soest, approximately 40 miles away, and was the primary facility for hospitalized soldiers. A local clinic provided basic medical care. Navigating these differences in infrastructure and operations was another eye-opening experience for me and my family.

During my time in Germany, I visited one of my soldiers hospitalized in Soest. All I knew was the hospital's location in the city, but finding it proved difficult. I stopped at a local police station and asked, "Do you speak English?" The officer sternly replied in German, "Nein." Realizing he wanted to test me, I switched to German and asked for directions to the Belgian hospital. That surprised him, and he promptly replied in English, "Go back past two traffic lights, turn left, and it will be on your right." I thanked him, smiled, and followed his directions, successfully locating the hospital. He simply wanted to push me to try speaking German, and I was prepared to do just that!

Shopping for groceries and supplies was another challenge. The local Post Exchange and Commissary were tiny, roughly the size of two large bedrooms. The commissary was restocked weekly on Thursdays, and customers lined up before it opened. If you weren't early, fresh meats and other essentials would be gone. Larger Post Exchanges and Commissaries were located in Gießen and Frankfurt, about two and a half hours away. These trips were reserved for every three to four months to stock up on necessities. Church services were held at the American School on base, keeping us connected to our faith and community.

We had the opportunity to visit Amsterdam, The Netherlands, a couple of times. These trips, organized by the Chaplain's Office, were a mix of culture and exploration. We saw traditional cheese-making demonstrations and marveled at the endless rows of tulips in the fields, displaying vibrant colors. It was fascinating to see ships on the horizon, appearing to sail above the land, as Holland lies below sea level, protected by its famous dikes. We also visited the Red Light District—a stark cultural experience—but unless you knew its reputation, there was no obvious indication of what was happening there.

Another memorable trip was to Austria. We explored the underground salt mines and visited Salzburg, a beautiful city rich in history.

During this trip, we encountered a bit of family drama. While in Salzburg, our youngest child, who was two at the time, had a bathroom emergency. My wife, accompanied by another couple, took her to the restroom. Meanwhile, I boarded the bus with our two older children, as it was scheduled to depart for Germany. The bus did not wait, leaving my wife and the others behind. They had to wait for the next bus back. Needless to say, my wife was not pleased with the situation.

A significant personal test occurred while stationed in Germany. I began experiencing back problems and was prescribed Tylenol with codeine. During a routine, unannounced drug test, my urinalysis came back positive. This initiated a formal process, including having my rights read to me—a deeply embarrassing experience as a Master Sergeant.

All positive tests were automatically retested using more advanced analysis, such as a mass spectrometer. While waiting for the results, I experienced a range of emotions, uncertain about what might happen. This period tested my resolve and character. Fortunately, the retest came back negative, clearing me of any wrongdoing. Although my faith was not as strong then as it is now, I now realize that God was watching over me. That experience reinforced my understanding of perseverance and trust, even during uncertain times.

After completing our tour in Germany, we were reassigned to Fort Hood, Texas (now Fort Cavazos). Once again, I returned to the 502d Adjutant General Company with duties at the SIDPERS Interface Branch. However, my time there was short-lived due to my rank as a Master Sergeant. The Adjutant General's office needed an experienced Administrative Noncommissioned Officer, and I was selected to fill that role.

Not long after, the First Sergeant position for the 502d became available, and the newly appointed Company Commander requested me to step into the role. As First Sergeant, I introduced innovations to enhance personnel management, creating a database for the company's soldiers. This database automated reports, significantly aiding the commander in maintaining accountability and monitoring personnel status.

During my tenure as First Sergeant, I achieved a major milestone—I was selected for promotion to Sergeant Major. Reflecting on my journey, I recall the doubts and criticisms from others. I've had a moustache since my mid-twenties, though it wasn't easy for me to grow one. The naysayers often linked my appearance and career progression to their biases.

First, they said I wouldn't be promoted to Master Sergeant without attending the NCOES Academy. I never attended but was still promoted. Then they claimed I wouldn't be selected for Sergeant Major unless I shaved my moustache and attended the Sergeant Major Academy. Again, I proved them wrong, earning the promotion without compromising my identity or values. When someone sarcastically remarked, "You must walk on water," I replied that my success came from staying motivated, exceeding expectations, and adhering to regulations for dress and appearance, leaving no room for discrimination. And by this time, my faith in the Lord had grown stronger. I knew I wasn't walking this journey alone—I had divine support.

As First Sergeant, I also dealt with challenging leadership. The Division Command Sergeant Major, a notoriously difficult individual with what many referred to as a "Napoleon complex," often targeted my company. He was perpetually dissatisfied, frequently complaining about the cleanliness of our area of responsibility. If he spotted even a few scraps of paper, he'd call me—often at home on weekends—demanding that I send soldiers to clean it up.

Initially, I tried to accommodate him, but there's a limit to patience. One weekend, after yet another call, I'd had enough. I firmly told him that if he wanted paper picked up, he could find someone else to do it. I was done.

When I became promotable to Sergeant Major, he wasted no time ensuring I was reassigned out of the Division. His effort to remove me didn't bother me in the slightest. As I left, I thought, *Good riddance! Don't blink, or you'll miss me leaving!*

My next assignment took me to the 546th Personnel Service Center, III Corps, at Fort Hood, Texas, where I was promoted to Sergeant Major and assigned as the 546th Personnel Service Center Sergeant Major. After two years in this role, army politics led to the 1st Cavalry Division G-1 Sergeant Major being reassigned to my position, so I had to vacate it. Shortly after, the III Corps Adjutant General Sergeant Major position became open, awaiting a replacement from overseas. Once the new Sergeant Major arrived, I was temporarily assigned as the III Corps G-1 Sergeant Major.

In this role, I had co-responsibility for coordinating the Soldiers of the Month and the Sergeant Morales Selectee Ceremony. If anything went wrong, my Sergeant and I would receive a stern reprimanding from the III Corps Command Sergeant Major, and it was never a pleasant experience. Though my assignment was temporary, I was also tasked with helping stand up the future personnel brigade, which would oversee all Personnel Service Companies. After six months, I was reassigned as the Personnel Sergeant Major for the 13th Corps Support Command.

One of my major responsibilities in this role was serving as the Manifest Officer for the deployment of units to Iraq during Operation Desert Storm. Regardless of the time of day or night, I was responsible for ensuring that all soldiers designated for deployment were present. I was given my own vehicle for the task, and I completed this mission successfully. As a result, I received a III Corps Support Command Coin. While I didn't fully appreciate the value of the coin at the time, it did seem to irritate my Officer in Charge, which I found amusing.

After the deployment, I received orders for my second assignment to Korea, this time with the 1st Infantry Division as the G-1 Sergeant Major. To prepare for this, I had to attend the Battle Staff School at Fort Bliss, Texas. While the training was mandatory, I didn't find it particularly useful, especially after arriving at my new position. It became clear that it was a role with little authority and minimal responsibility. The G-1 Officer didn't seem inclined to delegate any real power to me, so I spent most of my time doing work that felt important but ultimately had no impact.

Frustrated with the situation, I was ready to leave, and as if on cue, God came to my rescue. The Department of Defense announced a reduction in force, deciding that there were too many Sergeants Major in my specialty. The army implemented an early retirement program for a number of us, and when my name appeared on the list, I knew it was divine intervention. I had long felt the weight of racism and prejudice in that assignment, and God was delivering me from it.

The Commanding General requested that my Officer in Charge (OIC) and I report to him. When we arrived, he asked if I knew why I had been called in. I replied that I didn't. He then read aloud the cover letter regarding the reduction in force, followed by the letter from the Department of the Army ordering my early retirement. I simply said, "No, sir."

He seemed taken aback and asked, "You seem really calm. Do you understand what this means?" I replied, "Yes, sir." Then he asked, "You're not upset?" I responded again, "No, sir."

He paused and said, "Okay. Others didn't take this news the way you have. Is there anything you need to help transition from soldier to civilian life?" I told him, "No, sir." He nodded and said, "Alright then, you're dismissed." I saluted, thanked him, and left the office.

Once outside, my OIC asked if I had been expecting this. I replied, "No, sir." He was surprised and asked, "What are you going to do now?" I answered, "I'll be alright." He couldn't quite understand my calmness, but what he didn't understand was my faith and my trust in God. I didn't know exactly what God had planned for me, but I knew He was in control, and I trusted that my family and I would be fine.

Since I couldn't retire overseas, I was reassigned to Retirement Services at Fort Hood, Texas, where I officially retired after 26 years of military service.

UNEXPECTED JOURNEY

Chapter 6
Professional Life

After retiring from the U.S. Army, I sought employment with the Killeen Independent School District in Killeen, Texas. I was hired as a Level I Special Education Aide. After serving in that capacity for one year, based on my qualifications, I was upgraded to Level III. This was a good transition from a military mindset to a civilian community mindset. It was somewhat rewarding. I say somewhat because, due to the retainable ability of the students, it was difficult to see the value of my efforts. This did not enter into my commitment to the students. The important thing was that I could see the appreciation in the students for someone showing caring. The thing that was discouraging to me was seeing some of the teachers provoking the students to act out so that they could get them removed from the classroom.

When I went for my evaluation interview, I was asked how did I feel about the teacher/student relationship and interactions. Being one to stand for the truth, I shared how some teachers knew what buttons to push to get certain students to act out and get removed from the classroom. The person doing the interview told me that I could do something about it. I asked how. She said, "Go back to school and get a teaching degree, and come back and teach the students the right way." I took that to heart and decided to do just that. I enrolled at the University of Mary Hardin Baylor in Belton, Texas. With my credits from previous courses taken and my Associate Degree from Central Texas College, I graduated in two years with a Bachelor of General Studies with certification in Business Administration and Computer Information Systems. After passing the State of Texas Teacher Certification Tests, I was certified to teach in these two areas.

My student teaching was done in Computer Science at Killeen High School, Killeen, Texas. After doing several interviews at several middle and high schools, I served as a substitute teacher at Manor Middle School. I was waiting to hear back from the interviews. Neither one panned out. What I found out, though, was that I was not gifted to teach middle school. Shortly after this, the School District called me to go to Ellison High School to interview for the Computer Science Teacher position. I did, and the two assistant principals were overwhelmed by the interview and said that they were excited to offer the job to me. Of course, the principal, who was out of town, and the district had to approve. The next week, the district offered me a contract which I signed, and I taught Computer Programming there for the next nine years.

During my first two years, I was evaluated by the principal. I received the highest rating, not only as a new teacher but even among all teachers at the high school. I also was awarded Teacher of the Month. Because of my teaching methods and ability, many of the varsity football players were assigned to my class. While I was teaching there, I taught every quarterback. I also taught players that played in the National Football League. One in particular came to me from Alternative School. He was subdued and angry with trust issues. I was able to reach him by showing him that he was important and deserved to learn and that he could learn. He received that encouragement and became an A student. He went on to the University of Oklahoma and then to the NFL. Whenever he was in town, he would stop by to thank me for being patient with him and showing him that he could do it.

The most important thing about teaching is to show the students that you care and that you believe in them. Give them help and attention not only for things in the classroom but also show that you are open for recommendations and advice in life experiences. Not only one student will thank you, but many will come back and thank you. Then even other students that you did not teach will hear about it and trust your advice. I would not allow students to just give up. It surprised me that I had some students that did not show up for finals because they thought that they couldn't pass them. I literally called one student home and convinced him to come and take his finals. The assistant principals were informed, and they agreed with me. The student agreed to come in and take his final, and I stayed with him until he completed it. The other students were already gone. If he had not taken and passed the test, he would not have graduated. He did, and he did. The next year, he and another former student came back to the school. He wanted to come by but was embarrassed. The other students finally convinced him to come into my classroom. He came in, thanked me, and hugged me. The students in the classroom asked me, "Mr. Swint, is that your son?" He answered no, he was not my son. Everyone just laughed.

One of the things that teachers are not supposed to do is to become emotionally involved with the students. I will say this: if you are not a strong emotional person, if you are not a fully mature adult, if you cannot resist the temptations of sexually aggressive students, then you should not be in the classroom. I know that this can be a problem. During my time as a teacher, there were both male and female students who flirted with and came on to me. Because I knew who I was and what I was there for, there was no problem dismissing and resisting these overtures. Once I immediately shut this down, it didn't happen anymore. So when you hear or read in the news about a teacher/student sexual involvement, the teacher was not necessarily the one who initiated it. However, the teacher was responsible for being the one to shut it down.

In my ninth year, I began to experience some medical issues. I began to experience weakness. There were times when I had to climb stairs, and I had to approach this slowly. I didn't know what was happening, so I alerted the principal that I was led to requesting early retirement due to uncertainty of physical ability. He told me that it was God saying that it was time to be available for the assignment that He had for me. At this time, I was doing dual work. I was pastoring as well as teaching high school.

The VA Hospital in Temple, Texas recommended an appointment to a pharmacologist. I did, and after several lab tests, it was determined that the weakness was due to a lack of Vitamin D3 and being prescribed Statin medication. And sure enough, after starting to take 1000 IU of Vitamin D3, the physical weakness went away. I had already taken early retirement from teaching. I was now in full-time ministry.

Chapter 7
Spiritual and Ministerial Life.

My first memory of attending worship services was during a revival at Oak Grove Baptist Church in Sandersville, Georgia. The church building was about two miles away from our house, back in the woods. It has since been relocated to a housing community. It was our custom to walk to church. It was okay while it was daylight, but the service didn't end until dark. Walking home in the dark was certainly an experience. Of course, most everyone in the community walked, so we were not alone. No one was ever bitten by snakes. I didn't know then, but I know now that it was God who protected us.

I joined and was baptized at Bold Spring Missionary Baptist Church. That was my mother's family church. It was quite a distance from where we lived, probably at least eight or nine miles. I was twelve years old when I was baptized. We lived out in the countryside, or as it was called, the rural area. At the age of 18, we moved to town. We began attending St. Galilee Church of God in Christ (COGIC). My mother, two brothers, and a sister converted to this denomination. Although I attended, I did not join.

While I attended Fort Valley State University, I participated in Episcopalian Worship Services. During my time in the Army, I participated in Non-denominational Worship as well as COGIC Worship. It was during my time in Germany that I became really involved in the Worship Experience. After returning to the United States, I began to be more committed to worshipping the Lord. My wife and children had been members of Anderson Chapel African Methodist Episcopal Church. So when we returned to Fort Hood, I also united with Anderson Chapel. Seeing my commitment, I was appointed a Steward by Pastor M. C. Cooper. I served as a Steward and Secretary to the Official Board for the next seven years.

As I became more and more committed to service in the Kingdom of God, I began to feel a strange movement within me. I didn't understand

47

what was happening. During the worship experience, during praise and worship, I started feeling like something was trying to break out of me. This caused me to feel like I was outside my body watching strange things happening to me. I would have this dream that something was chasing me in the dark. There was a car, but I couldn't get it started to get away from whatever was chasing me. There was a man standing near the car, so I asked him how to get the car started. He said to me Proverbs 9:10. The next morning, I remembered the dream and got my Bible and read the scripture. It was then that I realized that something unusual was happening to me. It was at Bible Study one Wednesday that the Spirit took over me, and had me crawling on the floor crying my eyes out. The following Sunday, I surrendered to God and said, "Here I am, whatever you want me to do, I am willing."

My first sermon was based on the scripture, 2 Chronicles, Chapter 7, Verse 14: "If my people who are called by my name will humble themselves and pray, will turn from their evil ways, and seek my face, then I will hear from heaven, forgive their sins, and heal the land." The land needs healing! I received a license to preach on February 24, 1991, by Presiding Elder Rev. J. R. Anderson, was ordained as an Itinerant Deacon on October 17, 1993, and as an Itinerant Elder on September 10, 1995, by Bishop John Richard Bryant.

Also, on October 17, 1993, I was appointed pastor of Union Chapel AME Church, Cedar Creek, Texas, which is 90 miles from my home. However, the first church that I went to as temporary pastor was Center Union AME Church, Smithville, Texas. At the 10th District AME Church Planning Conference in November 1993, I received a permanent appointment to Center Union, which is 119 miles away. The congregation at Center Union were very nice people and were very good to us. The most notable thing about them was the 75- and 80-year-old women who did the yard work. We were like, "Wow, we'd never seen this before." The Homecoming and Church Anniversary was an unbelievable event. People came from all directions to that country church.

The church building of Union Chapel needed some restoration work done. It had also been vandalized. But the people were ready to do the work. And it was not long before it had been restored and was ready for worship service. These two churches were basically on the same route but 30 miles apart. This was before the time of modern hotels. Because of the distance, we would stay overnight in Bastrop, Texas. The hotel was not a thing of comfort, and places for eating were scarce. On New Year's Day, there were no places open for eating. There was a family that was members of Union Chapel that insisted on us going to have dinner with them. They were excellent at preparing food. The peach cobbler was a culinary masterpiece. So this is where we went following worship service. The two churches met every other Sunday for worship, alternating Sundays. I was at one or the other every Sunday.

After serving as pastor of Center Union and Union Chapel for two years, I was appointed pastor of Sauney Chapel AME Church, Chappell Hill, Texas. Sauney Chapel is 130 miles from my house. It is closer to the city of Houston than to my house. I served as pastor there for two years. The most interesting thing about Sauney Chapel is that they held a Fall Festival with horseback riding and hayrides. There were also different types of booths set up, such as face painting, dunking for apples, and others. This was mainly for the youth of the church and community. I can say that it was fun. It was the first and only time that I rode a horse. Driving to and from Sauney Chapel could be quite a challenge sometimes. On one particular Sunday, when we began the worship experience, the weather was cold but clear. By the time the services ended, it was snowing. It was no fun to drive 130 miles in the snow. By the time I was about 60 miles from home, the snow was four inches deep and still coming down. It was melting off the car and freezing along the edges. The highway became snow ruts. Driving was okay as long as I remained in the ruts left by the traffic in front of me. But God kept us and brought us through.

After two years of pastoral charge at Sauney Chapel, I received an appointment as pastor of Paul Quinn AME Church, Bastrop, Texas. Bastrop was 95 miles away. Up to this point, the churches that I pastored, including

Paul Quinn, were in the old West Texas Annual Conference. It no longer exists. It was at Paul Quinn AME Church that I got the opportunity to host an Annual Conference. The week before we were to host the conference, I received a call that there was water running out the front door, down the steps, and down the street. I was like, "Oh, wow, why now!" We were able to repair the pipe and restore the floors of the bathrooms, the floor of the foyer, and replace the foyer furniture. When the conference began, I informed the Bishop of what had happened. He said that God was baptizing and anointing the building, preparing it for the Annual Conference. The Annual Conference went fine! When I was appointed to the church, it was about to go into foreclosure. Thanks to God, we were able to stop the procedure and restore the financial status of the church. It was during my time at Paul Quinn Church that I started to become the finance person for the district.

One Sunday following the worship service, I went out of the sanctuary to the parsonage next door. As I stepped onto the porch, a snake came around the corner and started hissing at me. One of the trustees who came out behind me came over and took care of the situation. During that same week, I drove into my car garage at my house. I opened the car door and stepped out. A snake appeared in front of me. To this day, I am not sure if it came from under the car or out of the car. But it also challenged me. I said to myself that I must have made some demon mad and it tried to retaliate. Thank God the Lord was on my side.

While serving as pastor there, a situation came up about supporting a transportation request from the district. Many pastors in the district didn't think that the churches should do that since it was not a part of the assigned budget apportionment. But when it came to the day of reckoning, it was said that it was I who led the opposition. So the Presiding Elder requested that I be moved to another location. Sometime during the week prior to the 10th District Planning Conference, I had a dream about a man. It was an unusual dream. When I looked at the man from the front, everything seemed normal. But then there was a revelation. When I was shown the man from the back, there was nothing but an empty shell. This revealed to me that there was someone in the hierarchy of the district that had no spiritual constitution. There was no godly foundation there. There was a spiritual void in this person. This person was working in opposition to my ministry.

I was assigned as pastor to Allen Chapel AME Church, Taylor, Texas. Even with the unsolicited reassignment, you will notice a pattern of distances away from my house. Taylor is 55 miles away from my house. My pastoral charge at Allen Chapel lasted for six years. This was the longest time that I had been pastor of a church. It was during my pastoral charge at Allen Chapel that I became the District Treasurer and Administrator. When a vacancy occurred at a church with a classification one level up, I was moved and appointed pastor of Wesley Chapel, Georgetown, Texas. Georgetown is 40 miles from my house. Do you see a pattern in distance away? It was at Wesley Chapel where I was given the responsibility as Administrator, Treasurer, and Accountant. This included receiving all district funds and reports, depositing the funds, writing checks as required, and consolidating the reports and preparing other reports to submit to the 10th District Headquarters. It was also during this time that I was appointed as Treasurer for the Southwest Texas Annual Conference. Subsequently, I served as Treasurer for the Paul Quinn District, Stewardship and Financial Committee Chairman of the Northwest Annual Conference, and a member of the Tenth District Budget and Finance Committee. I was also appointed to the Stewardship and Finance Committee of the General Conference of The African Methodist Episcopal Church held in Orlando, Florida during July 2021.

Another peculiar thing happened to me while I was the pastor of Wesley Chapel, Georgetown. It was again following the worship experience that my wife and I were leaving the sanctuary on our way to a restaurant. As I turned onto the street near the church campus, a car ran a stop sign right in front of me. When I got to the main highway, a car made a U-turn in front of me. After we got to the restaurant, ordered our food, the server brought out the food and dumped it into my lap. I was like, really. What is this all about. Well, the good news is that our food was free after the new order was delivered! However, while being the pastor there, I heard directly from heaven at unexpected times. This again happened at a restaurant. We were having lunch again. A lady came up to us and asked me if she could give me a message from the Lord. Naturally, I said yes. She said that the Lord said the roadblocks have been moved out of your way. I thanked her and gave God praise. At another time, a voice said to me, "You no longer have to defend yourself." Again, I gave praises to God, and I began to preach with renewed freedom and power. Those whom the Son has set free are free indeed!

After being the pastor of Wesley Chapel for seven years, I began to see some unusual revelations. I refrained from talking about them because I did not know if I would speak them into existence. I will give an example later that seems like I did. On the Sunday following the Ecumenical Thanksgiving Worship Service, it rained. When we came out of the building, there was the brightest rainbow that I had ever seen. We all stood in amazement, gazing at the sky wondering what portent this could be.

It was during the 10th District Planning Conference in November 2016, while we were eating breakfast on the morning of the Closing Worship Service, that I received a phone call. It is at the Planning Conference that all remaining pastoral appointments are made. The call was from a number that I was not familiar with. I did not answer, and it went to voicemail. It was the Bishop requesting that I call her. I did as requested. She asked me if I was amenable to a move. I said yes. She then said it was closer to home, but not the main one. I readily understood what that meant. It meant that I wasn't being assigned to Anderson Chapel. Anderson Chapel was my home church. It was where I started my journey in ministry. However, she didn't say what church it was. So, I was left in suspense until the appointments were being read. When the pastor of Adams Chapel AME Church, Harker Heights, Texas, was appointed to a church in Waco, I knew then to which church I would be appointed. Sure enough, that was it. Adams Chapel is five miles from my house. Now, can you see the pattern? From Sauney Chapel, 130 miles away, to Paul Quinn Church, 95 miles away, to Allen Chapel, 55 miles away, to Wesley Chapel, 40 miles away, to Adams Chapel, five miles away. I served as pastor of Adams for six years. I had reached the mandatory retirement age of 75, so I had to retire at the Annual Conference in 2022.

After not being able to obtain financial aid and student loans for college tuition after graduating from high school, my decision was to embark on a career in the United States Army. I had not considered or imagined an additional career in ministry or as a teacher. This is why this truly was an Unexpected Journey!

Chapter 8
Reflections and Life Lessons

As I look back on my life, I see a journey full of struggles, hard work, and blessings. Every step I took brought me to where I am today. Life was never easy, but each challenge taught me something valuable. I want to share some of the most important lessons I have learned and how they shaped my path.

The first lesson is about perseverance. There were many times when life seemed unfair. Growing up in poverty, struggling in school, facing difficulties in the military, and adjusting to new responsibilities were all tough. But I never gave up. I kept moving forward, even when the road was unclear. I have learned that success is not about never falling but about getting up every time you fall.

I remember days when we had little to eat and nights spent studying by kerosene lamp. I faced rejection and failure, but I refused to let them define me. Perseverance is the ability to push forward even when everything seems against you. It is about keeping faith in yourself and in the possibilities ahead.

Another important lesson is the power of education. I started my education in a small rural school with very few resources. I had to work extra hard to prove myself. But education opened doors for me that I never imagined. It gave me confidence, skills, and opportunities to build a better future. No matter where you come from, knowledge can change your life.

Education is more than just learning facts—it is about developing discipline, critical thinking, and resilience. I met teachers who believed in me and friends who encouraged me. Learning became my escape from hardship and my gateway to success. It taught me that knowledge is a lifelong pursuit and that every lesson, whether in a classroom or in life, adds value to who we are.

Faith has been my guiding light. There were times when I felt lost or uncertain about what would happen next. My faith in God kept me strong. Through every challenge, I believed that He had a plan for me. Serving in ministry allowed me to share this faith with others. I have seen how faith can heal, guide, and inspire people. No matter what happens, believing in something greater than yourself can give you strength.

One of the hardest moments in my life was facing personal loss and uncertainty about my future. But prayer and trust in God provided me with peace. Faith is not just about religion—it is about hope, belief, and trusting that every hardship serves a purpose. It has given me the courage to take risks, to lead, and to help others find their own path.

Family is another great blessing. My childhood was filled with struggles, but I always had my family by my side. My mother worked hard to take care of us, and my siblings and I shared both joys and hardships. Later in life, my wife and children became my support system. Life is not just about personal success but about the people we share it with. Family is our foundation, and we must always cherish and support them.

I have learned that love, patience, and understanding make a family strong. In times of trouble, it is family that stands by you. Their support has been my greatest strength. Whether it was my mother's sacrifices, my wife's encouragement, or my children's love, each relationship has shaped me into who I am today.

Helping others is the key to a meaningful life. Whether through military service, ministry, or simple acts of kindness, I have found great joy in making a difference in others' lives. The world is full of challenges, but each of us has the power to bring change in small but meaningful ways. If we choose to help and uplift those around us, we create a better world for everyone.

Acts of kindness do not have to be grand. Sometimes, listening to someone, offering a word of encouragement, or sharing what little we have can mean the world to another person. In my years of service, I have seen how a small gesture can change lives. Giving is not about what we have but about the willingness to share.

As I move into the next phase of life, I do not know what the future holds. But I know that I will keep learning, growing, and helping others. I hope my journey serves as a reminder that no matter where you start, you can achieve great things with faith, hard work, and determination.

To those reading this, I encourage you to never stop believing in yourself. Life will throw challenges at you, but each challenge is an opportunity to grow. Stay strong, stay faithful, and never stop moving forward. Your journey may be unexpected, but it can still lead to amazing places.

Thank you for taking the time to read my story. I hope it has inspired you in some way. May your own journey be filled with hope, strength, and blessings. Life is full of twists and turns, but each experience makes us stronger. Keep pushing forward, embrace every challenge, and always remember, you are capable of greatness.

Chapter 9
Challenges and Overcoming Hardships

Life is full of challenges. Some are expected, and others come out of nowhere. From my early years in poverty to facing discrimination, struggling in school, and dealing with hardships in the military, I have had my share of battles. But through it all, I learned that faith, resilience, and determination can push a person through even the toughest situations.

One of my first battles was poverty. As a child, I did not understand why we had less than others. I only knew that we had to work harder for everything. Simple things like shoes, school supplies, and even food were not guaranteed. We often ate what we could grow or gather. Hand-me-down clothes were normal. While other kids might have worried about playing, I was learning the value of making do with what we had.

School was another challenge. Not because I struggled with learning, but because being poor made me a target. Bullies came after me because I did well in class. I was called names, teased, and even physically attacked. But I refused to let their words and actions stop me. Instead, I used my education as my way out. I knew that if I wanted a better life, I had to push through the struggles and stay focused.

Growing up in the South as a Black boy in the 1950s and 1960s meant I had to deal with racism. There were places I could not go, things I could not do, and opportunities that were out of reach simply because of my skin color. I remember going to town and noticing that white people had better schools, cleaner stores, and nicer homes. At a young age, I started to ask, "Why is it like this?"

Even when I joined the military, racism was present. Promotions were harder to get, and respect was not always given freely. I had to work twice as hard to prove myself. There were times when I felt like giving up, but something inside me refused to quit. I knew that if I stopped fighting, I would be giving in to what others expected. Instead, I pushed harder, learned more, and made sure that no one could deny me based on race alone.

The military is known for its discipline and order, but it is also a place where you face tough physical and mental challenges. When I first joined, the training was brutal. I had to push my body beyond its limits. There were days when I thought, "I can't do this anymore." But I remembered my struggles growing up, and I knew that if I survived those, I could survive this.

The biggest challenges were not always physical, though. There were moments when leadership decisions seemed unfair. There were times I was overlooked for promotions or placed in situations where I had to prove my worth repeatedly. The pressure was high, and the responsibility was even higher. But through all these struggles, I learned one important lesson:

"You can either let challenges break you or let them shape you."

I chose the second option.

Chapter 10
Lessons from Leadership and Service

Leadership is not about power or position. True leadership is about service, responsibility, and setting an example. My journey from a young boy in Georgia to the highest enlisted rank in the military, and later to a senior pastor, taught me valuable lessons about what it means to lead.

One of the first lessons I learned as a leader was that you cannot lead others if you cannot lead yourself. The military teaches discipline, but I had already learned it growing up. Waking up early, working long hours, and never complaining were things I was used to. But leadership required more. It meant making hard decisions, being responsible for others, and staying strong even when things got tough.

One of my biggest tests came when I was placed in charge of a group that did not respect me at first. Some thought I was too strict. Others felt I did not belong in that position. But instead of trying to be liked, I focused on earning their respect. I led by example, working harder than anyone else, making fair decisions, and ensuring that no one was left behind. Over time, they saw that I was not just their leader, but someone they could trust.

In both the military and ministry, I realized that leadership is not about standing above others, but standing with them. A good leader does not just give orders—he serves. In the military, this meant looking out for my team, making sure they had what they needed, and standing up for them when necessary.

In ministry, it was no different. A pastor is not just someone who preaches on Sunday. A pastor is someone who listens, guides, and supports people through their hardest times. Whether in the military or the church, I knew that serving others was my true calling.

One mistake many people make is thinking that leaders have all the answers. The truth is, the best leaders never stop learning. Even after years in the military, I still learned new things every day. Even after years in the ministry, I found that God always had something new to teach me.

Leadership is a journey, not a destination. And the moment you stop growing is the moment you stop leading.

Chapter 11
Faith and Personal Transformation

If there is one thing that has guided me through every stage of life, it is my faith. Faith has been my foundation, my comfort, and my strength. Without it, I do not know where I would be today. It has shaped my decisions, carried me through hardships, and given me a purpose far greater than I could have imagined.

I did not always understand God's plan for me. When I was a child, faith was something I heard about often but did not fully grasp. My mother and grandmother would remind me that "God will provide," and we prayed together as a family. But as a young boy, I often questioned why we had to struggle. I would see other kids wearing new clothes and shoes while I had to make do with whatever we could afford. There were nights when I went to bed hungry, and I wondered why God allowed it.

Growing up in poverty teaches you many lessons. It teaches you to appreciate the little things, to be resourceful, and to find joy in what you have rather than what you lack. But it also creates deep struggles. I remember the shame I felt when my classmates made fun of my old shoes. I remember how hard my parents worked to put food on the table, sometimes skipping meals themselves just to make sure we had enough. I remember watching my mother pray late into the night, asking God to take care of us.

At the time, I did not understand why life was so hard. But looking back, I see that every hardship was teaching me something valuable. It was teaching me resilience. It was teaching me to trust in God even when I did not see a way forward.

One moment that stands out in my memory was a Saturday morning when I was about ten years old. We had no food in the house, and my mother were trying to figure out what to do. My mother, as always, turned to prayer. She gathered us in the kitchen, and we held hands as she prayed for God to provide. I remember feeling doubtful—how could prayer put food on our table? But just a few hours later, a my sister's dad knocked on our door with a bag full of groceries.

I will never forget that moment. It was the first time I truly saw faith in action. It was as if God had heard our prayers and answered them directly. That day, I began to understand that faith was not just about going to church or reading the Bible—it was about trusting that God was always working, even when we did not see it.

But faith does not always come easily, especially for a child. As I grew older, I started asking more difficult questions. If God loved us, why did we have to suffer? Why did bad things happen to good people? Why were some people born into wealth while others had to struggle for every meal?

These were questions that did not have easy answers. I struggled with them throughout my teenage years. But over time, I began to see that faith is not about having all the answers—it is about trusting that God has a plan, even when we do not understand it.

Life did not get easier as I grew older. In fact, the challenges only became greater. My transition from childhood to adulthood was filled with trials that tested my faith in ways I never expected.

One of the hardest things I had to face was the reality of racism and discrimination. Growing up as a Black youth in the country, I quickly learned that the world was not always fair. There were times when I was treated differently because of my skin color. There were opportunities that were denied to me, not because I lacked ability, but because of prejudice.

At first, I felt anger. I wondered why God allowed such injustice. But over time, I realized that my faith was not meant to shield me from hardship—it was meant to give me the strength to endure it. I turned to God in prayer, asking for guidance. Instead of letting racism break me, I let it make me stronger. I worked harder. I proved myself. I showed the world that my worth was not defined by others' opinions, but by God's purpose for me.

One particular moment that tested my faith happened during my early adult years. I had applied for a job that I was more than qualified for, but I was denied the position. I knew the reason—it had nothing to do with my abilities and everything to do with the color of my skin. I felt defeated. I wanted to lash out. I wanted justice. But instead of letting bitterness consume me, I turned to God.

I remember sitting alone in my room, praying with all my heart. I asked God for strength, for patience, and for wisdom. And in that quiet moment, I felt a deep peace wash over me. It was as if God was reminding me that no man could take away what He had planned for me. That experience changed my perspective. Instead of seeing closed doors as failures, I started seeing them as redirections. I began to trust that God had something better in store for me, even if I could not see it yet.

When I joined the military, my faith was tested in new ways. The military is a place of discipline, structure, and resilience, but it is also a place where you face unimaginable hardships.

There were times when I was physically exhausted, pushed beyond my limits, and expected to keep going. There were moments when I had to make life-or-death decisions under pressure. There were times when I saw fellow soldiers struggling, broken by the weight of war and responsibility.

During my time in the military, I learned that faith is not just for church on Sundays—it is something you carry with you every single day. It is what keeps you going when you feel like you have nothing left.

One of the most difficult moments in my military career was when I lost a close friend in battle. It was a devastating loss, and for the first time in a long time, I questioned everything. Why would God allow such a good man to die? Why did some people make it home while others did not?

I struggled with these questions for a long time. But through prayer, I found peace. I realized that life is fragile and unpredictable, but God is constant. Even in the darkest moments, He is there. That realization gave me the strength to keep going, to honor my fallen friends by living a life of purpose.

Chapter 12
A Boy with Big Dreams

Dreams don't always come from what you see around you—sometimes, they come from what you lack. Growing up in Sandersville, Georgia, I didn't see success, wealth, or power in my everyday life. What I saw were hard-working people trying to survive. My family was among them. But deep inside, I believed I was meant for something more.

We lived in a simple house with no electricity, no running water, and no luxuries. Our days were filled with chores—chopping wood, hauling water, working in the fields. Life was predictable: you worked, you ate if you had food, and you did it all over again the next day. But my mind was always somewhere else.

I would lie awake at night, staring at the dark ceiling, thinking about a future beyond the fields. I didn't know exactly what that future looked like, but I knew it was different from what I had.

As a child, I found ways to escape, even if only in my mind. I listened to older folks tell stories about people who had "made it." I watched men in uniform when they came to town, imagining what it would be like to be respected. I paid close attention to preachers at church, fascinated by their powerful words.

One of the first moments I realized I wanted more was during a Saturday trip to town. While my mother focused on shopping, I studied the people around me. I watched businessmen in pressed suits and teachers who spoke with confidence. These men had control over their lives, and I wanted to be like them.

Dreaming was one thing; surviving was another. I was smaller than most boys my age, which made me an easy target for bullying. Some kids teased me for being smart; others picked on me just because they could. I fought back when I had to, but more than anything, I wanted to prove myself through success.

School was my refuge. I enjoyed learning because I knew education was my way out. My teachers noticed my potential, and some went out of their way to help me. Their belief in me fueled my own determination.

But even with that support, the journey wasn't easy. We were poor—so poor that sometimes I went to school without lunch. Some teachers helped me in small ways, slipping me extra food or finding ways to make sure I was taken care of.

Still, I refused to let my situation define me. I worked hard, studied harder, and kept my dreams alive.

I didn't know how or when, but I was determined to break free from the cycle of poverty. I wanted to do something meaningful with my life. That belief carried me forward through every struggle, pushing me toward the life I knew I was meant to have.

Chapter 13
Lessons from the Land

Life as a sharecropper's child was not easy, but it taught me everything I needed to survive. Before I ever wore a uniform or stood behind a pulpit, I learned discipline, responsibility, and resilience from the land.

We didn't own the land we worked on. My family, like many others, farmed land that belonged to someone else. At the end of the harvest, the landowner took his share, and we were left with barely enough to get by. It was an endless cycle—one that kept us in poverty no matter how hard we worked.

As children, we didn't have a choice. We worked the fields, planting, weeding, and harvesting. There was no complaining—only doing what had to be done.

From a young age, I had responsibilities that most children today couldn't imagine. I learned to chop wood, carry water, and tend to crops. My hands were calloused before I was old enough to fully understand why life was so hard.

One of my earliest lessons in responsibility came when I was trusted to gather firewood. I was just a boy, but that small job meant warmth for my family. If I didn't do it, we would be cold.

I also learned about sacrifice. Sometimes, my mother went without food so that we could eat. There were days when all we had were cornbread and molasses. But even in those tough times, we found ways to be grateful.

The land taught me patience. Crops didn't grow overnight; they took time, care, and effort. Life was the same way—success wouldn't come instantly, but through persistence.

It also taught me respect. Nature was powerful. A dry season could ruin everything. A storm could wipe out weeks of work. Those lessons stayed with me long after I left the fields.

At the time, I didn't realize how much these experiences would shape me. But when I look back, I see that the hardships of my childhood prepared me for leadership, service, and faith. The discipline I learned in the fields helped me rise through the military ranks. The patience I gained from farming guided me in my spiritual journey.

Even though life as a sharecropper's child was tough, I wouldn't trade those lessons for anything. They made me who I am.

Chapter 14
Turning Points

Every journey has key moments that change its direction. For me, there were several turning points—decisions and experiences that led me from a struggling boy in the countryside to a man of leadership and faith.

One of the biggest turning points was when I left home. It was a terrifying step. Up until then, everything I knew was in the countryside. But deep down, I knew I couldn't grow if I stayed.

Leaving meant taking risks. It meant stepping into the unknown. But it also meant opportunity.

The military was another major turning point. It gave me structure, purpose, and a sense of identity. For the first time in my life, I wasn't just another poor boy from Georgia—I was part of something bigger.

At first, the discipline was tough. The training pushed me beyond my limits. But the same work ethic I had learned as a child helped me rise through the ranks. I listened, learned, and applied myself.

The military also taught me leadership. I learned how to make decisions under pressure, how to take responsibility, and how to lead by example.

Perhaps the most significant turning point was when I felt the call to ministry. I had always been drawn to leadership, but I never imagined myself as a pastor. Yet, as I grew in faith, I realized that my life experiences—both the struggles and the successes—had been preparing me to serve others.

Answering the call wasn't easy. It required sacrifice, humility, and a willingness to step outside my comfort zone. But looking back, I see how every challenge, every lesson, and every turning point led me to where I was meant to be.

Chapter 15
From Soldier to Pastor

Life is a journey filled with unexpected twists and turns. When I first joined the military, I never imagined that one day I would stand before a congregation, delivering sermons, guiding people in their faith, and serving as a spiritual leader. My goal at the time was simple: to serve my country, gain stability, and build a future for myself. But looking back, I realize that every challenge, every hardship, and every experience in the military was preparing me for a greater purpose—becoming a pastor.

Growing up in a small town in Georgia, life was tough. I came from a poor background, where hard work was a necessity, not a choice. My early years as a sharecropper's son taught me the value of perseverance, discipline, and faith, even before I fully understood what those words meant. When I joined the military, I carried those lessons with me. At first, I thought the army would be just another job—something to provide financial stability and structure to my life. But over the years, I realized that it was shaping me in ways I could not yet comprehend.

The military gave me purpose at a time when I needed direction. I learned about leadership, responsibility, and resilience. I experienced hardships that tested my faith, moments of fear that made me pray harder, and encounters with fellow soldiers who needed guidance and support. Without knowing it, I was already doing the work of a pastor—I was just doing it in a different setting.

In the early days of my service, the physical and mental challenges were overwhelming. The training was intense, the expectations were high, and the pressure was constant. But I embraced it because I knew that strength was built through struggle. Every obstacle prepared me for something greater. I learned to wake up before dawn, march for miles with heavy equipment, and function under extreme conditions. I learned that leadership was not just about giving orders but about inspiring and guiding those who depended on me.

One of the most defining moments in my transition from soldier to pastor came when I found myself stationed far from home. I remember a particular night when exhaustion weighed heavily on me—not just physical exhaustion, but emotional and spiritual fatigue. I sat alone, staring into the darkness, reflecting on my life. In that quiet moment, I felt a deep stirring in my heart. I realized that my purpose extended beyond the military. It was a realization that I had been prepared for something else—something even more significant.

At first, I ignored this feeling. I told myself that I was a soldier, not a preacher. I continued my duties, leading my fellow soldiers, training new recruits, and fulfilling my responsibilities. But the thought never left me. Over time, I found myself drawn to spiritual conversations. I started attending church services more frequently, reading the Bible with deeper interest, and seeking out chaplains to ask about their experiences.

Many of my fellow soldiers confided in me about their struggles— fear, doubt, homesickness, and the emotional burden of military life. I listened to them, comforted them, and prayed with them. Without realizing it, I had stepped into a pastoral role long before I ever stood behind a pulpit.

As my military career progressed, the feeling that I was meant for something more became stronger. The transition was not easy. I had spent years dedicating myself to the military, and the idea of stepping away from that life was overwhelming. But I knew that my experiences in the army had given me something priceless—discipline, leadership skills, and the ability to guide others. These were not just military qualities; they were qualities of a strong and effective pastor.

When I finally left the military and stepped into ministry, I realized that I was not abandoning my past—I was building on it. The discipline I had learned helped me stay committed to my spiritual journey. The leadership skills I had developed allowed me to guide my congregation with confidence and wisdom. The resilience I had gained helped me handle the challenges of ministry with strength and patience.

Being a pastor was not without its difficulties. Leading a congregation required more than just faith; it required patience, understanding, and the ability to navigate people's struggles. But I was prepared. The military had trained me to handle pressure, to think clearly in difficult situations, and to lead by example.

As I look back, I see that my journey from soldier to pastor was not a random shift—it was a calling. Every experience in the military was shaping me for this role, even when I did not realize it. My life had come full circle. I had gone from leading soldiers in battle to leading people in faith. The weapons had changed, but the mission remained the same—to serve, guide, and protect.

Now, as a pastor, I use my experiences to help others. I understand hardship, sacrifice, and struggle because I have lived through them. I know what it means to feel lost and uncertain because I have been there. But I also know that with faith, determination, and a willingness to follow God's plan, anything is possible.

Chapter 16
Wisdom for the Next Generation

Life is a journey, and like any journey, it is filled with lessons. Some of these lessons are learned through personal experience—through the trials and triumphs that shape us. Others are passed down to us by those who have walked the path before us, offering guidance, encouragement, and wisdom. As someone who has lived through poverty, served in the military, and led as a pastor, I have gathered a wealth of insights that I feel compelled to share with the next generation. The world you are growing up in is vastly different from the one I knew as a young person, but the core principles of life remain unchanged. Success, fulfillment, and purpose are still rooted in timeless truths that transcend generations.

In this chapter, I want to share with you the lessons I have learned, not as a perfect man, but as someone who has stumbled, fallen, and risen again. My hope is that these words will inspire you, challenge you, and equip you to navigate the complexities of life with courage and wisdom.

I was born into poverty. My family had little to no financial resources, and the future was uncertain. There were no guarantees, no silver spoons, no safety nets. But even as a child, I knew that my circumstances did not have to define my destiny. I made a decision early on that I would not let my background limit my potential. I would work hard, stay disciplined, and keep pushing forward, no matter how difficult the road became.

This mindset—this refusal to be defined by my starting point—has been one of the most important factors in my life. It is a lesson I want to impress upon you: Your background does not determine your future. Your mindset does.

The world often tells us that success is reserved for those who are born into privilege, who have access to the best schools, the best connections, and the best opportunities. But history is filled with stories of people who started with nothing and achieved greatness. What set them apart was not their circumstances, but their determination to rise above them.

Consider the story of Oprah Winfrey, who was born into poverty in rural Mississippi. She faced countless obstacles, including abuse and discrimination, but she refused to let her circumstances define her. Through hard work, resilience, and an unwavering belief in herself, she became one of the most influential women in the world. Her story is a testament to the power of mindset.

Young people today face their own set of challenges. The world is more competitive, more fast-paced, and more demanding than ever before. But the principle remains the same: Success is not about where you start; it's about where you are willing to go. It's about the choices you make, the effort you put in, and the vision you have for your life.

In a world that values instant gratification, the concept of hard work can seem outdated. We live in an age where people want quick results— overnight success, viral fame, and shortcuts to wealth. But the truth is, real success comes from persistence. It comes from showing up every day, even when the work is hard, even when the results are not immediately visible.

I learned the value of hard work at a young age. Growing up in poverty, I had to work for everything I had. There were no handouts, no easy paths. But those early experiences taught me a valuable lesson: Effort and dedication are what separate those who achieve their dreams from those who give up too soon.

Whether you are in school, starting a career, or pursuing personal growth, hard work is the foundation of success. It's not enough to have talent or potential; you have to be willing to put in the effort to develop that talent and realize that potential.

Consider the story of Michael Jordan, widely regarded as one of the greatest basketball players of all time. What many people don't know is that Jordan was cut from his high school basketball team. Instead of giving up, he used that failure as motivation to work harder. He practiced relentlessly, honing his skills and pushing himself to be better. His work ethic, more than his natural talent, is what made him a legend.

The same principle applies to every area of life. Whether you are studying for an exam, building a business, or working on a personal goal, success requires effort. There will be days when you feel like giving up, when the work seems too hard or the results too far away. But it is in those moments that you must dig deep and keep going. Remember, the road to success is not a sprint; it's a marathon.

Throughout my life, faith has been my anchor. In times of struggle, it gave me strength. In times of doubt, it gave me clarity. And in times of despair, it gave me hope. Faith reminded me that I was never alone, that even when I couldn't see the path ahead, God had a plan for me.

For me, faith is not just about religion; it's about trust, resilience, and believing in something greater than yourself. It's about knowing that there is a purpose to your life, even when the journey is difficult.

Young people today face a world that is often uncertain and chaotic. The pressures of school, work, and relationships can feel overwhelming. In times like these, faith can be a source of comfort and strength. It can remind you that you are not alone, that there is a bigger picture, and that your struggles are not in vain.

Faith also teaches us humility. It reminds us that we are not in control of everything, and that's okay. Sometimes, the most important thing we can do is trust—trust in God, trust in the process, and trust in ourselves.

In my years as a soldier and a pastor, I have seen many people rise to positions of power and influence. But I have also seen many of them fall, not because they lacked talent or intelligence, but because they lacked integrity. They compromised their values, made unethical choices, and lost the trust of those around them.

Integrity is more valuable than any title or achievement. It is the foundation of trust, respect, and credibility. Your reputation can change overnight, but your character is what truly defines you.

Integrity means doing the right thing, even when no one is watching. It means being honest, even when it's hard. It means staying true to your values, even when the world around you is telling you to compromise.

In a world that often values success at any cost, integrity can seem like a rare commodity. But it is one of the most important qualities you can cultivate. It is what will set you apart, not just as a professional, but as a person.

One of the greatest lessons I have learned is that true fulfillment comes from serving others. Whether it's helping a friend, supporting a community, or dedicating your life to a cause, service brings purpose and meaning to life.

A selfish life is an empty life. The happiest and most successful people are those who give more than they take. They understand that their success is not just about what they achieve for themselves, but about how they impact the lives of others.

Service can take many forms. It can be as simple as lending a listening ear to a friend in need, or as grand as dedicating your life to a mission that helps others. Whatever form it takes, service is a powerful way to connect with others, make a difference, and find purpose.

I have failed many times in my life. I have made mistakes, faced setbacks, and experienced disappointments. But each failure taught me something valuable. Each one made me stronger, wiser, and more resilient.

Failure is not the end; it's a stepping stone to success. The key is to learn from your mistakes, get back up, and keep moving forward. Every great success story includes failures along the way.

To the next generation, I say this: Be strong, work hard, stay true to your values, and never stop believing in yourself. The road ahead will not always be easy, but with faith, determination, and wisdom, you can achieve

76

anything. Life is a journey, and every step, no matter how difficult, is leading you toward something greater.

Chapter 17
Gratitude and Humility

Life is a journey filled with ups and downs, victories and defeats, joys and sorrows. Along the way, I have learned that two qualities have the power to transform even the most difficult moments into opportunities for growth: gratitude and humility. These two virtues have been my guiding lights, helping me navigate challenges, stay grounded in success, and appreciate the people who have supported me along the way. In this chapter, I want to share how gratitude and humility have shaped my life and why they are so important for anyone seeking a meaningful and fulfilling journey.

Gratitude is more than just saying "thank you." It is a way of seeing the world, a mindset that focuses on the good even when things are hard. Growing up in poverty, I could have easily focused on what I didn't have. But my mother taught me to be grateful for what we did have—a roof over our heads, food on the table, and each other. That lesson stayed with me throughout my life.

When I joined the military, there were times when the training was grueling, and the conditions were tough. I remember one particularly difficult exercise where we were out in the field for days, with little sleep and limited food. It would have been easy to complain, but instead, I chose to focus on the things I was grateful for: my health, my teammates, and the opportunity to serve my country. That shift in perspective gave me the strength to keep going.

Gratitude doesn't mean ignoring the challenges or pretending everything is perfect. It means finding the silver lining, no matter how small. When I faced setbacks in my career or personal life, I reminded myself of the lessons I had learned from my mother. I focused on the people who believed in me, the skills I had gained, and the opportunities that still lay ahead. Gratitude gave me the courage to keep moving forward, even when the path was uncertain.

Humility is the quality of recognizing that we are not the center of the universe. It is about understanding that our achievements are not just the result of our own efforts but also the support, guidance, and kindness of others. Throughout my life, I have been blessed with many successes—rising to the highest enlisted rank in the military, becoming a Senior Pastor, and building a family I am proud of. But I have always tried to remain humble, knowing that these achievements were not mine alone.

In the military, I learned the importance of humility early on. No matter how high I rose in rank, I never forgot that I was part of a team. I relied on the skills and dedication of my fellow soldiers, and I made sure to listen to their ideas and concerns. I knew that true leadership was not about commanding respect but earning it through humility and service.

As a pastor, humility became even more important. Leading a congregation is not about being in charge; it's about serving others and helping them grow in their faith. I have always tried to approach my role with a humble heart, knowing that I am not perfect and that I have as much to learn from my congregation as they do from me. Humility has allowed me to connect with people on a deeper level, to understand their struggles, and to offer support without judgment.

Throughout my life, I have been blessed with countless acts of kindness and support from others. These moments have reminded me that no one succeeds alone, and that we all need help from time to time. One story that stands out to me is from my early days in the military. I was a young soldier, far from home and feeling overwhelmed. One of my superiors noticed that I was struggling and took the time to sit down with me, offering advice and encouragement. That small act of kindness made a huge difference in my life, and it taught me the importance of paying it forward.

Another story that comes to mind is from my time as a pastor. There was a family in my congregation who was going through a very difficult time. They had lost their home in a fire and were struggling to rebuild their lives. The community came together to support them, donating clothes, food, and money. I was amazed by the generosity and compassion of the people in our church. It was a powerful reminder that we are all connected, and that even the smallest acts of kindness can have a big impact.

These stories have shaped my understanding of gratitude and humility. They have shown me that no matter how much we achieve, we are never truly self-made. We are all part of a larger community, and it is through the support and kindness of others that we are able to succeed.

One of the most important lessons I have learned is the importance of giving credit where it's due. Too often, people are quick to take credit for their successes but slow to acknowledge the contributions of others. I have always tried to do the opposite. Whether it was in the military, in my career, or in my ministry, I made it a point to recognize the efforts of those around me.

In the military, I made sure to commend my fellow soldiers for their hard work and dedication. I knew that our success as a team depended on each person doing their part, and I wanted to make sure that everyone felt valued and appreciated. As a pastor, I have always tried to highlight the contributions of my congregation, whether it was through a kind word, a note of thanks, or a public acknowledgment during a service.

Giving credit where it's due is not just about being fair; it's about building trust and fostering a sense of community. When people feel appreciated, they are more likely to give their best effort and to support one another. It creates a positive cycle of encouragement and collaboration that benefits everyone.

Gratitude and humility are not just virtues; they are ways of living. They remind us to appreciate the good in our lives, to stay grounded in our successes, and to recognize the contributions of others. They teach us that we are part of something bigger than ourselves, and that our journey is shaped by the people we meet along the way.

As I look back on my life, I am filled with gratitude for the many blessings I have received and for the people who have supported me. I am also humbled by the opportunities I have had to serve others and to make a difference in their lives. My hope is that by sharing these lessons, I can inspire others to embrace gratitude and humility in their own journeys.

Life is not always easy, but with gratitude and humility, we can find meaning and joy in even the most challenging moments. We can build strong relationships, create a sense of community, and leave a positive legacy for future generations. And in the end, that is what truly matters.

Chapter 18
The Power of Community

Life is not lived in isolation. From the earliest days of my childhood to my years as a pastor, I have learned that community is the foundation of a meaningful and fulfilling life. Whether it was the small, close-knit neighborhood where I grew up, the tight bonds formed in the military, or the loving congregation I served as a pastor, community has always been a source of strength, support, and growth. In this chapter, I want to explore the role of community in my life, how it has shaped me, and why it is so important for all of us to build and nurture relationships with others.

The Role of Community in My Life, From Childhood to Ministry

I was born into a small, rural community in Sandersville, Georgia. Life was simple, but it was also deeply connected. Everyone knew everyone, and people looked out for one another. My family didn't have much, but we were rich in relationships. Neighbors helped each other with farming, shared food during hard times, and came together for celebrations and church services. That sense of belonging stayed with me throughout my life.

As a child, I didn't fully understand the importance of community, but I felt it. When we walked to church together, when we gathered for revival services, or when we helped a neighbor in need, I felt a sense of unity and purpose. Those early experiences taught me that we are stronger together than we are alone.

In the military, I saw the power of community in a different way. The bonds formed between soldiers were unbreakable. We trained together, worked together, and relied on each other in life-and-death situations. The military taught me that trust, respect, and collaboration are essential for any group to succeed. It wasn't just about following orders; it was about being part of a team that had each other's backs.

When I became a pastor, I saw community in a new light. The church was more than just a place of worship; it was a family. People came together to support one another, to celebrate joys, and to mourn losses. As a pastor, I had the privilege of being part of those moments, of helping people connect with each other and with God. I saw how a strong community could transform lives, offering hope, healing, and a sense of belonging.

How Communities Come Together in Times of Need

One of the most beautiful things about community is how it comes together in times of need. I have seen this time and time again, both in my personal life and in my ministry. When someone is struggling, the community rallies around them, offering support, encouragement, and practical help.

I remember a time when a family in our congregation lost their home in a fire. It was a devastating loss, but the community stepped up in an incredible way. People donated clothes, furniture, and money. Some offered temporary housing, while others helped with the rebuilding process. It was a powerful reminder that no one has to face hardship alone. When we come together, we can overcome even the toughest challenges.

In the military, I saw this same spirit of unity. During difficult missions or when a fellow soldier was injured, the team would come together to support one another. We shared the burden, both physically and emotionally, and it made us stronger. Those experiences taught me that community is not just about sharing the good times; it's about standing together during the hard times.

The Importance of Building and Nurturing Relationships

Building and nurturing relationships is at the heart of community. It's not enough to simply be part of a group; we have to actively invest in the people around us. This means showing up, listening, and being there for others, even when it's not convenient.

In my life, I have tried to prioritize relationships. Whether it was with my family, my fellow soldiers, or my congregation, I made an effort to connect with people on a deeper level. I learned that relationships are built on trust, honesty, and mutual respect. It's about being willing to give as much as you receive, and sometimes even more.

One of the most important lessons I've learned is that relationships take time and effort. They don't happen overnight, and they require constant care. But the rewards are worth it. Strong relationships bring joy, support, and a sense of belonging. They remind us that we are not alone, and that we have people who care about us and believe in us.

Community is not just about individual relationships; it's also about working together toward a common goal. Collaboration is the key to collective growth, and I have seen this in every stage of my life.

In the military, collaboration was essential for success. We had to work together, communicate effectively, and trust each other to get the job done. I learned that when people come together with a shared purpose, they can achieve incredible things. It's not about individual glory; it's about the success of the team.

As a pastor, I saw the power of collaboration in a different way. The church was a place where people with different talents and skills came together to serve a greater purpose. Whether it was organizing events, helping those in need, or spreading the message of faith, we achieved more together than we ever could have alone.

Collaboration also teaches us humility. It reminds us that we don't have all the answers, and that we can learn from others. It encourages us to listen, to be open to new ideas, and to value the contributions of everyone in the group. When we collaborate, we grow not just as individuals, but as a community.

Final Thoughts on the Power of Community

Community is one of the greatest gifts we have in life. It gives us strength, support, and a sense of belonging. It teaches us the value of relationships, the importance of collaboration, and the power of coming together in times of need.

As I look back on my life, I am grateful for the communities I have been part of—from the small, rural neighborhood where I grew up, to the military, to the church. Each one has shaped me in different ways, and each one has taught me important lessons about connection, compassion, and collective growth.

My hope is that we all recognize the power of community and make an effort to build and nurture relationships with those around us. Whether it's through family, friends, work, or faith, we all have the opportunity to create communities that uplift, inspire, and support one another. And in doing so, we can make the world a better, more connected place.

About The Author

Silas Swint is an African American man whose journey began in the heart of central Georgia. Raised by a single mother, Silas was instilled with a sense of determination and resilience from an early age. Growing up in a challenging environment, he quickly learned the importance of hard work, faith, and perseverance. Despite the difficulties that life threw his way, he never allowed his circumstances to define him.

A dedicated student throughout his life, Silas always sought to expand his knowledge and improve his economic standing. His thirst for learning was driven by an inner belief that knowledge was the key to breaking through the barriers that often seemed insurmountable. The word "cannot" was foreign to him, and he viewed any challenge as an opportunity for growth rather than an obstacle to his success. This mindset has guided him through countless hurdles, allowing him to see setbacks as temporary and not defining of his potential.

As a child, he learned that the word "no" was not a roadblock, but a challenge to find another path. Whether it was in school, relationships, or his career, Silas was never deterred by rejection or adversity. He developed an unwavering belief in his own abilities, always finding creative and resourceful ways to overcome challenges.

At the core of Silas's journey is his deep faith in God. He credits his perseverance and strength during difficult times to his belief that with God, all things are possible. This unwavering faith has been his foundation, providing him with the courage to push through moments of doubt and uncertainty. His trust in a higher purpose and divine guidance has allowed him to face life's most trying times with grace and fortitude, and it continues to be the driving force behind everything he does.

Silas's experiences, both in overcoming personal struggles and striving for success, are reflected in his writing. His first book, *Unexpected Journey*, is a testament to his life's journey—one marked by resilience, faith, and the constant pursuit of a better tomorrow. Through his words, he hopes to inspire others to believe in themselves and to never give up,

no matter the challenges they face. He believes that anyone, regardless of their background, has the power to transform their life and create the future they desire.

When he's not writing, Silas enjoys such as traveling, reading, or community involvement], which help fuel his creativity and keep him grounded.

Silas Swint

UNEXPECTED JOURNEY

www.ingramcontent.com/pod-product-compliance
Lightning Source LLC
Chambersburg PA
CBHW051329120626
46547CB00016B/2464